With over twenty years of experience in computing education, **Shahneila Saeed** has seen the changes to the computing curriculum from many perspectives. As a teacher and Head of Department, she led her department's transition to computing several years ahead of government changes. As one of the founding members of the Computing at School board, she helped develop the Computing Programmes of Study.

In 2014, Shahneila joined Ukie (UK Interactive Entertainment Association) to become Head of Education and Director for the nationwide Digital Schoolhouse programme. She is the author of *Hacking the Curriculum: Creative Computing and the Power of Play,* a book that uses play-based learning to teach computing skills and concepts.

Develop Your Child's Computing
Skills Without Spending Any Money

How to RAISE A TECH Genius

SHAHNEILA SAEED

ROBINSON

ROBINSON

First published in Great Britain in 2020 by Robinson

13 5 7 9 10 8 6 4 2

Copyright © Shahneila Saeed, 2020

The moral right of the authors has been asserted.

A CIP catalogue record for this book
is available from the British Library.

ISBN: 978-1-47214-362-4

Typeset in Sentinel Light by Hewer Text UK Ltd, Edinburgh
Printed and bound in Great Britain by Clays Ltd, Elcograf S.p.A.

Papers used by Robinson are from well-managed forests and other responsible sources.

MIX

How To Books are published by Robinson, an imprint of Little, Brown Book
Group. We welcome proposals from authors who have first-hand experience
of their subjects. Please set out the aims of your book, its target market
and its suggested contents in an email to howto@littlebrown.co.uk

All activities in this book have been developed by the author and contributing teachers who are part of the Digital Schoolhouse programme. Sincerest thanks for their contributions, inspiration, expertise and support to

Jane Adamson
Estelle Ashman
Chris Baker
Steve Bunce
David Eley
Tony Gilbert
David Wicks

Ukie's Digital Schoolhouse together with Nintendo UK is a not-for-profit programme which enables academic institutions (Schoolhouses) to deliver creative computing workshops to local primary schools. Pupils can experience a unique approach to play-based learning through innovative activities and free, adaptable resources. Underpinned by evidence-based research and combined with ground-breaking careers education, the programme successfully bridges the gap between academia and industry, to ensure pupils are aptly equipped for the future digital economy.

Contents

Introduction: Why is this all so important?

To say that we are living in a digital age is unlikely to surprise anyone. Technology has infiltrated virtually every aspect of our lives and is so inherent in our world that often we simply don't 'see' it. Artificial Intelligence is on the rise and visibly so. Personal AI assistants such as Alexa, Siri and Cortana are no longer confined to being a gimmick feature on our phones, but can now provide real assistance in our homes. From controlling our lights and electronic devices to reordering our shopping, these home devices do all that and so much more. Ask Alexa to tell you a story or Siri to tell you a joke and each will provide a humorous interaction.

Technology continues to grow at such an incredible rate that we can only begin to imagine the possibilities it might bring and what the world will look like in just ten years. Driverless cars as a mass-market product are now on the horizon. How long will it be before the Amazon Echo develops arms, legs and a digital face? Eye-tracking technologies and 3D printing are among the many technologies that are already providing life-changing solutions for people who need physical assistance. It won't be long before this existing tech is refined, repackaged and made available more widely. The sci-fi movies of yesterday are fast becoming today's reality.

And that's exciting, incredibly exciting in fact. Perhaps even more fascinating are our children's natural assumptions of what technology can do.

You can see today's toddlers wonder why their home TVs don't respond to touch. Having a toy bot that you can programme with voice commands is as natural to children today as plastic dolls were to us yesterday.

With technology booming the number of jobs and opportunities within the tech sector is on the increase. You'd think that given young people's natural inclination towards technology there would be more applicants for roles than positions available. Unfortunately, though, that's the conundrum. Despite our children's interest and appreciation of tech, most of them aren't opting to choose a career within the industry, meaning technical positions are a challenge to fill. As a result, there are shortages, and this is known as the digital skills gap. For some companies, more than 40 per cent of staff are recruited from overseas. Why? Because there simply aren't enough students with relevant digital skills coming through the education system here in the UK.

But why is that? You wouldn't naturally look at the students of today and think that would be the case. It is a huge concern and one that is actively being addressed within both the education and tech sectors.

In 2016 the World Economic Forum published 'The Future of Jobs', a report which looked at the skills that will be needed in the twenty-first-century economy. It is true that AI technology threatens a lot of roles with automation, but it is also true that the same technology will create numerous new roles and positions to help manage and further develop this automation. Likewise, the roles that aren't at risk are those that require human insight, innovation and creativity. Some jobs may go but many more jobs will change. The truth is this: unless we prepare our children for the shifting world, they will struggle. Unless we help them develop their creativity and problem-solving skills along with a love for lifelong learning and resilience they will struggle to adapt in the constantly shifting digital world of tomorrow.

Most jobs today require at least some minimal use and understanding of digital devices; digital skills are the fourth literacy and just as important as reading, writing and arithmetic. It is critical, therefore, that we prepare our children for the jobs of today and the world of tomorrow.

So yes, learning computing and programming (or coding) is important. Its importance has been recognised not only by industry and educators but also by government itself. So much so in fact that in 2014 it became a mandatory part of the curriculum for all children from the age of five.

So, what are our children learning in school?

All children that attend a state-funded school have to be taught the computing curriculum from Year 1 through to Year 11. The programmes of study set down the key principles that pupils should be taught during each Key Stage. They cover the full breadth of computer science and digital literacy and include creative media development and online safety.

*A high-quality computing education equips pupils to **use computational thinking and creativity to understand and change the world**. Computing has deep links with mathematics, science and design and technology, and provides insights into both natural and artificial systems. The core of computing is computer science, in which pupils are taught the principles of information and computation, how digital systems work and how to put this knowledge to use through programming. Building on this knowledge and understanding, pupils are equipped to use information technology to create programs, systems and a range of content. Computing also ensures that pupils become digitally literate – able to use, and express themselves and develop their ideas through, information and communication technology – at a level* *suitable for the future workplace and as active participants in a digital world.*

National Curriculum in England: Computing
programmes of study (September 2013)

The highly ambitious computing curriculum places computational thinking and creativity at its heart. These two concepts underpin the entire computing curriculum and encourage digital creativity and play-based learning. The change impacts all children from ages five to sixteen. But why is it so important?

As defined by Jeannette Wing, computational thinking is 'a way of solving problems, designing systems, and understanding human behaviour by drawing on the concepts of computer science.'[1] It is a set of cognitive thinking skills that can help us solve problems more effectively. So much of the modern workplace is about solving problems, whether it's a small problem to enhance business efficiency or developing a breakthrough product for consumers. Even if you're not involved in programming, chances are you will be involved in solving problems in some way.

We will unpick the details of the programmes of study and computational thinking in the next section, but what needs to be said here is that it's the approach that is important.

What are our children doing in their free time?

Whatever your answer to this question, it more than likely involves at least some element of 'play'. Play in its broadest sense is freeform and enables children to use their imagination and creativity, to have fun.

1 Wing, J. M., 2006, 'Computational thinking.' *Communications of the ACM*, 49, 33–35. https://www.ncbi.nlm.nih.gov/pmc/articles/PMC2696102/

There may or may not be rules involved, and if there are, they may change – the play is not fixed; the point is to have fun. We know very young children learn through play. Pre-schools and nursery schools do this job extremely well and children are often taught about colours, numbers and letters through games, songs and other fun interactions. Arguably we continue to learn through play throughout our entire lives. While the mechanics of play and its nature may change over time, the essential ingredients and the demand that it is 'fun' do not.

As parents and educators we can use this. We can continue to use playful techniques to teach our children and in so doing develop within them a love for lifelong learning, creativity and innovation. Computing can be taught in the same way, and indeed that is the aim of this book. There is a common belief and practice that a person's first step to learning programming needs to be done in front of a computer screen with lines of code displayed. While that works for many, for others it can be an intimidating and daunting prospect.

With this book we aim to show how computing concepts and computational thinking can be introduced *without* the use of computers, using the games you may typically already be playing with your child. As a working parent myself I know just how busy our lives can be. Between juggling childcare responsibilities with our other commitments, there is very little time to spare for much else. If on top of that we feel that we have to learn programming before we are able to teach or support our children with it, then it simply won't get done. The nature of each of the activities within the book enables parents to play and learn *and have fun* alongside their children. Using commonly found household items, guided discussions and exploratory playful mechanics, each activity introduces you to one or more key computing concepts and ideas. By the time you've finished this book not only will your child have been introduced to key skills and concepts within computing, but fingers crossed they'll also be helping out with a household chore or two!

CHAPTER 1

Unpicking the National Curriculum for Computing

The National Curriculum in England for Computing is a statutory programme of study (PoS) that all state-funded schools need to follow. It applies right through from Key Stage 1 (starting at Year 1) to Key Stage 4 (ending with Year 11). Independent schools and Academies are exempt from having to follow this, but you will find that a lot of schools choose to do so anyway. The PoS outlines the subject content that needs to be taught at each phase of education. It does not, however, dictate how much time should be allocated; that is individually determined by each school.

In this chapter we will endeavour to explain at an introductory level the different elements of the curriculum and what they mean. Before doing so, it is worth remembering that the curriculum is focused around the core principles of computing, and as such does not contain specific references to technology. The guidance given to schools is for them to choose the best technology at their disposal to illustrate the concept being described. For example, you won't see any references to tablet devices or mobile phones, but understanding how a computer works internally, and how it sends and receives data from other computers is covered (this could then be taught using tablet devices and mobile phones).

PURPOSE OF STUDY

A high-quality computing education equips pupils to use computational thinking and creativity to understand and change the world. Computing has deep links with mathematics, science and design and technology, and provides insights into both natural and artificial systems. The core of computing is computer science, in which pupils are taught the principles of information and computation, how digital systems work and how to put this knowledge to use through programming. Building on this knowledge and understanding, pupils are equipped to use information technology to create programs, systems and a range of content. Computing also ensures that pupils become digitally literate – meaning they are able to use, and express themselves and develop their ideas through, information and communication technology – at a level suitable for the future workplace and as active participants in a digital world.

The definition of computing here is not limited to what we may typically understand as pure 'computer science'. Rather it is an amalgamation of the discipline that is computer science alongside digital literacy and information technology. It is important for children to have an understanding of how computers work and how to program them, but also how to use the tools that they provide to their advantage. Through understanding the world of technology around us, our children can learn how they can best harness its power to solve problems, innovate and express themselves. So, being able to create digital media and use the internet responsibly is covered alongside learning core programming skills.

Thinking skills are incredibly important, and you'll have seen the term 'computational thinking' being used. Thinking skills will be covered in more detail in the next section and are important to understand as they are at the heart of the PoS alongside creativity.

AIMS

The national curriculum for computing aims to ensure that all pupils:

- ◆ can understand and apply the fundamental principles and concepts of computer science, including abstraction, logic, algorithms and data representation;
- ◆ can analyse problems in computational terms, and have repeated practical experience of writing computer programs in order to solve such problems;
- ◆ can evaluate and apply information technology, including new or unfamiliar technologies, analytically to solve problems;
- ◆ are responsible, competent, confident and creative users of information and communication technology

---

Broadly, in everyday speak, the Programme of Study aims to help children:

- ◆ understand the concepts and principles of computer science and its components
- ◆ be able to analyse problems using computational thinking and to have practical experience of programming solutions to problems
- ◆ be able to evaluate their use of technology and apply their knowledge to solve problems
- ◆ to use technology safely and responsibly

The following sections outline the subject content as defined in the PoS. The numbered referencing is my own and has been added for clarity. The original PoS can be found on the government website.[2]

Key Stage 1 (KS1)

Pupils should be taught to:
1. understand what algorithms are; how they are implemented as programs on digital devices; and that programs execute by following precise and unambiguous instructions

An algorithm is a precise set of rules or instructions for performing a specific task. Children should understand what an algorithm is, ideally by being able to read and recognise pre-written algorithms as well as constructing their own. Children also need to understand that these algorithms can then be implemented onto computers as computer programs. In order to do anything, a computer will execute a program and follow a precise and unambiguous set of instructions.

1.1. create and debug simple programs

Be able to write a simple computer program. For five-year-olds this doesn't need to be any more complex then telling a robot to move three steps forward and one step right to reach an object. For example, a common type of robot used in schools is called the Bee-Bot, which is in the shape of a bee and can be programmed by pressing the arrow

2 https://www.gov.uk/government/publications/national-curriculum-in-england-computing-programmes-of-study

keys on its back to tell it what direction to go in. These Bee-Bots can be used in combination with playmats and different scenarios.

Debugging refers to removing the 'bugs' in the program, i.e. bits of faulty program code. So, imagine for example that a child programmed their Bee-Bot to go three steps forward and one turn right to reach the library, but they ended up at the bakery instead. You'd ask the child to look at their code and try to work out where it went wrong. Maybe they entered one step too many? Or turned left instead of right?

Essentially this is about being able to write and correct simple computer programs.

1.2. use logical reasoning to predict the behaviour of simple programs

---

Can they use logic to work out what an algorithm or computer program will do before it is executed? Maybe they've been given some instructions that draw a square. Can the child accurately read the instructions and predict that the outcome will be a square?

1.3. use technology purposefully to create, organise, store, manipulate and retrieve digital content

---

This is not necessarily about programming. This is the use of wider technology to be able to create, organise and manipulate information. The key learning here is being able to use and navigate technology comfortably, understand how to save their work, search the internet, Word-process a story, record a video, etc.

1.4. recognise common uses of information technology outside of school

1.5. use technology safely and respectfully, keeping personal information private; identify where to go for help and support when they have concerns about content or contact on the internet or other online technologies

Technology is not restricted to school. What technology do children experience outside of school? This may be the smartphones that their parents have at home but can also include their ability to recognise technology as they are out and about.

Online safety is an important factor to consider, and you'll see this strand being repeated throughout the key stages. The key learning here is for children to be able to use technology safely, to learn respect, for example not to damage other people's work or make hurtful comments online. However, it also includes teaching them ways to keep their personal information safe, and how to react and find help if something untoward was to happen.

Key Stage 2 (KS2)

2.1. design, write and debug programs that accomplish specific goals, including controlling or simulating physical systems; solve problems by decomposing them into smaller parts

In KS2 children begin to build upon their simple understanding of algorithms and programs. They begin to develop these with a sense of purpose. At Key Stage 2 children may well be introduced to how we can write programs to control physical objects. LEGO WeDo, Raspberry Pi, Crumble and Micro:bits are popular hardware items often used in schools here. However, lots of toy manufacturers have also released products that achieve a similar purpose. The game Scottie Go for example is a physical board game that also uses apps on your tablet device.

The concept of decomposition is formally introduced within the curriculum for the first time (although it may well have been covered earlier). Decomposition is the ability to take a problem and break it down into smaller chunks to make it more manageable and easier to solve. For example, when tackling a jigsaw puzzle you may choose to construct different sections first and then put them all together to form the complete puzzle. Decomposition is a computational thinking skill and will be covered later during that section.

> 2.2. use sequence, selection and repetition in programs; work with variables and various forms of input and output

Sequence, selection and repetition are programming concepts, as is the concept of variables. Children will be introduced to these concepts using graphical, block-based programming environments such as Scratch and Blockly.

The term 'sequence' refers to when instructions are written in a particular order such as 'A, B, C', one after the other. Selection introduces the concept of 'IF' – IF this criterion is true, THEN do this, ELSE it is false so do this. This is a conditional statement that enables a computer program to branch out and do different things. We can also find this concept in our everyday lives. For example, 'IF' it is raining THEN take my umbrella, ELSE leave home without it.

Repetition works when you tell the computer to repeat a set of instructions a specific number of times rather than having to write it out again and again. For example:

```
Repeat 4 times
    Forward 10 cm
    Right 90 degrees
End Repeat
```

The above algorithm draws a 10cm-sided square.

2.3. use logical reasoning to explain how some simple algorithms work and to detect and correct errors in algorithms and programs

---

Building upon KS1, children are to be taught to use their logical reasoning skills to be able to read and understand pre-written algorithms, to be able to explain their purpose and how they work as well as being able to spot and correct errors.

Being able to read and understand algorithms and code is an important step in the learning process towards becoming proficient programmers. Just as we learn to read and recognise words and sentences before we learn to write stories, it is useful to learn to read and understand algorithms and code before trying to write them. Being able to recognise when code doesn't 'make sense' and consider what corrections might need to be made are all part of the learning process here.

2.4. understand computer networks including the internet; how they can provide multiple services, such as the world wide web; and the opportunities they offer for communication and collaboration

2.5. use search technologies effectively, appreciate how results are selected and ranked, and be discerning in evaluating digital content

Networks are to be introduced for the first time in Key Stage 2. Understanding how computers communicate with each other and are able to send information across great distances is an underpinning concept that unlocks children's ability to understand a large part of the technology that surrounds us. The internet is a global network that impacts almost all areas of our lives, from banking and retail to smart homes including the use of smartphones, smart TVs and home AI assistants such as Alexa and Google Home.

It's safe to say that almost anyone can go to Google and type in a word or a phrase that they want to do a search for. And while Google tries its best to ensure you get the results you are looking for, there are simple clever techniques that we can use to ensure that we get the best results as quickly as possible. Understanding how search engines operate enables our children to manipulate the tools to help them get to the results they are looking for quickly and effectively. However, we can't always trust what we see online; it's important to be able to evaluate the content that we see to be able to identify whether or not it is from a trusted source. This strand helps children begin to be able to distinguish effectively between results.

2.6. select, use and combine a variety of software (including internet services) on a range of digital devices to design and create a range of programs, systems and content that accomplish given goals, including collecting, analysing, evaluating and presenting data and information

This strand is about the broader uses of technology. Children should be able to choose and combine the software they need to accomplish a given goal or solve a problem effectively. This could be for a range of tasks, including collecting and analysing data or presenting information. As an example, work within this area might be anything from filming their own video on the history of the Vikings to using a spreadsheet to analyse data collected from various sensors around their school, such as the thermometers in the school greenhouse.

2.7. use technology safely, respectfully and responsibly; recognise acceptable/unacceptable behaviour; identify a range of ways to report concerns about content and contact

Online safety is an important part of the school curriculum and as such features at every Key Stage. At Key Stage 2 students should be introduced to a range of tools and methods that they can use to report concerns as well as being able to identify an increasing range of acceptable and unacceptable behaviour.

Key Stage 3 (KS3)

From Key Stage 3 upwards the subject increases in complexity. It builds upon the foundations developed during Key Stage 1 and Key

Stage 2, but dives deeper, enabling students to have a significantly better understanding of the subject.

It is not within the scope of this book to explain in full detail each of the PoS statements below. However, these have been included here so that you can see how the subject progresses as children get older. Some top-line introductory explanations have been provided to aid understanding.

---

3. Pupils should be taught to:

3.1. design, use and evaluate computational abstractions that model the state and behaviour of real-world problems and physical systems

3.2. understand several key algorithms that reflect computational thinking (for example, ones for sorting and searching); use logical reasoning to compare the utility of alternative algorithms for the same problem

3.3. use two or more programming languages, at least one of which is textual, to solve a variety of computational problems; make appropriate use of data structures (for example, lists, tables or arrays); design and develop modular programs that use procedures or functions

---

At this stage students should begin to design and create their own computer programs. It is recommended that students explore real-world problems that they can relate to, and create their own computer models of how they work.

Computational thinking is also specifically covered here, including the teaching of several key algorithms that may or may not demonstrate how computers search or sort data. Encouraging students to develop their logical reasoning skills and consider alternative approaches to solving the same problem is also recommended. One solution may be more effective under certain circumstances but not others; evaluating solutions is a key computational thinking skill that is an important part of development.

During primary school, students will mostly have used graphics or block-based programming environments (with some exceptions – some primary teachers may choose to introduce Python to Year 6 students, but this is not mandatory). As they move into secondary school, teachers need to ensure that students are introduced to a text-based programming environment. This is quite often Python, but may well be a language such as JavaScript (it is worth checking with the computing teacher so you know what they plan to use). While a lot of schools start Year 7 students with the graphics-based programming environments, by Year 9 it is expected that they will understand the key programming concepts and be able to use them within a text-based language.

3.4. understand simple Boolean logic [for example, AND, OR and NOT] and some of its uses in circuits and programming; understand how numbers can be represented in binary, and be able to carry out simple operations on binary numbers [for example, binary addition, and conversion between binary and decimal]

3.5. understand the hardware and software components that make up computer systems, and how they communicate with one another and with other systems

3.6. understand how instructions are stored and executed within a computer system; understand how data of various types (including text, sounds and pictures) can be represented and manipulated digitally, in the form of binary digits

---

It is important for us to understand how computers work internally. What is the CPU? What do gigahertz and megahertz represent and why are they important things to consider when we are choosing a computer? How do computers store and manipulate data? Being able to understand that computers store all files, including software, photographs, videos and more in binary will help students get a better grasp of the technology around them. Understanding the basics of data representation and machine architecture will enable us to get a better grasp of how to manipulate the data and use it to our advantage.

3.7. undertake creative projects that involve selecting, using and combining multiple applications, preferably across a range of devices, to achieve challenging goals, including collecting and analysing data and meeting the needs of known users

3.8. create, reuse, revise and repurpose digital artefacts for a given audience, with attention to trustworthiness, design and usability

3.9. understand a range of ways to use technology safely, respectfully, responsibly and securely, including protecting their online identity and privacy; recognise inappropriate content, contact and conduct and know how to report concerns

These statements are deliberately broad, but essentially are about getting creative with technology. They encourage students to explore a range of digital technologies. This could be anything from developing their own YouTube films, to the next award-winning game, and everything in between. Developing a sense of audience and purpose is essential here. Encouraging students to think about 'why they are making that video' and 'who will watch it' will help them to tailor both their content and presentation.

Online safety is once again featured. It covers not just students' protection of their own online identities and being able to use technology safely, but also responsibly. Understanding that hacking and breaking copyright are both illegal and irresponsible are key aspects of being a responsible citizen in our digital world.

Key Stage 4 (KS4)

All pupils must have the opportunity to study aspects of information technology and computer science in sufficient depth to allow them to progress to higher levels of study or to a professional career.

4. All pupils should be taught to:

4.1. develop their capability, creativity and knowledge in computer science, digital media and information technology

4.2. develop and apply their analytic, problem-solving, design and computational thinking skills

4.3. understand how changes in technology affect safety, including new ways to protect their online privacy and identity, and how to identify and report a range of concerns

Key Stage 4, the GCSE years, but also the shortest section. It is expected that all students will have the opportunity to develop and refine their skills further and deepen their understanding of the subject matter. It is hoped that most students would do this by undertaking a relevant qualification, for example GCSE Computer Science. Every qualification has its own subject specification which maps out the subject delivery in great detail.

However, many students do not choose to follow a related qualification, and for those who don't it is expected that the school makes provisions for them to be able to develop these skills in their lessons. This may be delivered as a discrete subject, or through other subjects, such as Science, Maths or Art.

CHAPTER 2

A Brief Introduction to Computational Thinking

The working definition of computational thinking that most academics currently subscribe to was proposed by Jeannette Wing in 2006:

> *Computational thinking builds on the power and limits of computing processes, whether they are executed by a human or by a machine. Computational methods and models give us the courage to solve problems and design systems that no one of us would be capable of tackling alone ... Most fundamentally it addresses the question: What is computable? ... computational thinking is a fundamental skill for everyone, not just for computer scientists. To reading, writing, and arithmetic, we should add computational thinking to every child's analytical ability.*
>
> *Wing (2006)*[3]

Computational thinking is a set of skills that we can use to help solve problems effectively. Being able to think logically and algorithmically sit at its core, as well as an understanding of people. Utilising this diverse set of skills, which includes aspects such as team working and communicating clearly and concisely, is central to what computer scientists do. While the precise breakdown of these skills is still subject to some debate, here is what is commonly agreed:

---

3 Wing, J. M., 2006.

- Logical reasoning
- Algorithmic thinking
- Abstraction
- Decomposition
- Generalisation
- Evaluation

Logical reasoning

Logical reasoning enables us to make sense of problems by analysing existing facts and thinking about these in a clear and logical manner. We often use logical reasoning to make sense of all sorts of things, from the everyday problems that life throws at us to puzzles and games such as Sudoku and Plants vs. Zombies.

In computing, we ask our learners to use logical reasoning when they are testing and debugging their programs. Through logical reasoning we can often employ the other computational thinking techniques such as abstraction, decomposition and algorithmic thinking.

Algorithmic thinking

Algorithmic thinking is arriving at a solution to a problem and devising the steps necessary to implement it. Another way to think of an algorithm is as a series of instructions or steps to solve a problem. Thought of in this way, we realise that steps to solve problems or instructions can be found all around us, in our everyday lives as well as in other subjects, for example, when following a precise method for a science experiment, or following a recipe for a dish. We use algorithms in maths, and even PE teachers will give us the instructions we need to follow when we are learning a new sport.

Good instructions are clear, precise and follow a logical order that leads the person following them to solve the problem. Algorithmic thinking is one of the fundamental thinking skills behind programming. Good programmers are able to think algorithmically. But, described in this way, we can see that algorithms can apply to a range of circumstances, not just computer programs.

If we begin to think of algorithms simply as a set of well-defined instructions, we can then begin to develop some interesting and engaging activities around them.

Generalisation

Generalisation is looking at the algorithms that we have developed to identify patterns. Can we spot any patterns and find ways to describe them? Doing so would allow us to adapt our algorithm – our solution – to a wider range of problems. For example, we often generalise our (recipe) algorithms as we become more proficient at cooking. Consider this example: you've learned to cook a dish, it might be a pasta bake or a Thai curry. It may take several attempts before you've perfected your recipe or algorithm for this dish. Once you've picked up one, the next time you might try a different pasta or curry recipe. Before long, you realise that each time you cook a pasta or curry dish there are lots of things in common with the other times – patterns in the way the dish is made, that you spot. Before long, you've picked up on those patterns and you use them to make your own variations. So now you're able to make a pasta dish that you've invented or a curry of your own choosing, without needing to follow the original recipe that you've learned. You'll have changed things according to your own taste experiments along the way, but what you have done is generalised. You used your original recipe, spotted the key patterns, then made variations to come up with your own completely brand-new dish.

I bet you didn't realise you were such a talented computer scientist!

Abstraction

Abstraction is another key thinking skill and often follows on from generalisation. When describing a concept, idea or solution we can make it easier to explain by hiding any unnecessary complexity to reduce the details. Abstraction is yet another key skill that we use in so many ways and in so many subjects. For example, you might ask your child 'Are you ready for school tomorrow?' Your child will know that this question includes things like, is my homework done, is my bag ready, is my uniform ready and so on. If this is a question that you ask regularly, then you do not need to go into all the details every time. In computing, pupils creating and playing their own computer game would be an abstraction that hides the complexities of the game mechanics underneath.

> *Art is the elimination of the unnecessary.*
>
> Pablo Picasso

Abstraction is important as it makes problems easier to think about. There is a skill in it, it's important to choose the right details to hide without losing important information. One popular example is the use of models. Consider a map. A map is a model of a system. That system might be a city, a theme park or the London Underground. If we use London as an example, there are several maps available. You can get a road map of London, as well as the London Underground map, plus special tourist maps. If I was a tourist for a day, a special tourist map would help me plan what attractions I was going to visit, but I'd use the London Underground map to help me plan how I was going to get from the first attraction to the second. Likewise, the road map may be the best option out of the three if I was going to plan the route I was going to take while driving from home to my new place of work. Each map is an abstraction of London. They all provide slightly different information as different details have been hidden. For example, the tourist map may not display all the many small side streets in London, but they are all suitable for their purpose.

Being able to understand and use abstractions is a key computational thinking skill and often combines with generalisation and decomposition.

Decomposition

Decomposition simply means to break an idea, problem, solution or system down into smaller parts. Each part can then be dealt with and solved independently, thereby making larger systems easier to deal with. Pupils constructing products in Design & Technology use this thinking skill all the time. They often have to look at an item, for example a chair, and break it down into its smaller parts like its legs, seat, backrest and so on. Each part can then be individually designed and adapted.

Decomposition allows large and complex systems to be developed simultaneously by teams of people. For example, consider popular games such as the Assassins Creed series, FIFA or even Candy Crush. These are large and complex games and are developed over years by teams of people. Decomposition enables the game to be broken down into its component parts. There will be a group of artists responsible for creating all the in-game artwork, as well as sound engineers, programmers and many more. Each person will have their own set of responsibilities. Yet, when we play the game we see a single product.

Evaluation

Evaluation is a thinking skill you are likely to be familiar with already. In schools we ask pupils to evaluate the effectiveness of their work all the time. The only thing to remember here is that in computing we are often looking at the effectiveness of algorithms. Does the algorithm do the job it is intended to do? Is it fast enough? Is it fit for purpose? A chef will evaluate their recipe by testing it first. They will follow their recipe to make the dish and taste it when it's done. At that point they will consider the taste of the dish – do spices need to be added, for instance – as well as how long it took to make. They may also consider whether the recipe is easy enough for other chefs to follow without making mistakes. The answers to these questions will help them adapt and further improve their recipe as required.

LET'S PLAY . . .

What follows in the subsequent chapters is a number of activities that you can play with your child(ren) to help you both develop an understanding of key computing concepts. Each activity has been developed by a highly experienced teacher who is part of the Digital Schoolhouse programme. These teachers use playful learning techniques to teach computing to children across a range of ages.

Each activity is broken down into:

◆ What you need – the materials you need in order to deliver the activity. All the items listed will be ones commonly found around the home. Don't have what's listed? Try it with an alternative instead
◆ Recommended age range
◆ Prior knowledge or experience required
◆ Activity description – what to do
◆ What you are learning – an explanation of the key concept areas being taught through this activity
◆ Extending this – where next? A suggestion of activities that you could do to extend the learning here. These may link to digital activities that can be carried out either on a portable device or PC/laptop. Any software recommended is free and open-source. Where payable resources are recommended it will be because at the time of going to print a free-to-use version was not available
◆ Useful related online resources
◆ Activity sheets (if relevant)
◆ Answers to worksheet activities (if relevant), which can be found at the end of the activity

The activities are grouped by key topic areas. These are foundational topic areas that the subject is commonly divided into and this is the grouping most commonly used by qualifications-awarding bodies. Categories covered in this book are:

◆ Algorithms
◆ Data representation
◆ Logic
◆ Memory and storage
◆ Programming
◆ Security
◆ Systems architecture

······················

CHAPTER 3

Algorithmic Thinking

COLOUR SEQUENCE: FOLLOWING INSTRUCTIONS IN A SEQUENCE

What you need:
- ◆ Twister mat
- ◆ Pack of printed cards with coloured circles on
- ◆ Pack of printed cards with circles and directions
- ◆ Figures to move across the mat (optional)

Recommended age range:
Suitable for young children who know their colours

Prior knowledge/experience:
Your child must be able to recognise colours

What to do

Put the mat out onto the floor and make sure you have a pile of the coloured circle cards.

The challenge is to move a figure from one point to another point at the opposite side of the mat – see example below.

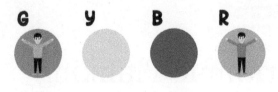

G = green Y = yellow
B = blue   R = red

1. Discuss the colours that are going to be landed on to get from one point to another. The example above shows that the character starts on green and the aim is to get to the red circle. Start with green, then go to yellow, blue and red.

2. Put the character at a different start and end point at opposite sides of the mat. This time take the coloured cards from the pack that the character needs to step on and put the colours in order. Follow the sequence of cards to test your sequence. Is there a different way to take your character from the start to the end point? Try a different start and end point.

Note: You can use anything for a character to move across the twister mat – a doll, a cuddly toy or even yourself!

What you're learning

You are learning to create and follow simple instructions as a method for introducing the concept of algorithms.

Link back to the National Curriculum for Computing:

Pupils should be taught to:

KS1

♦ Understand what algorithms are; how they are implemented as programs on digital devices; and that programs execute by following precise and unambiguous instructions.

♦ Create and debug simple programs.

KS2

- ◆ Design, write and debug programs that accomplish specific goals, including controlling or simulating physical systems; solve problems by decomposing them into smaller parts.
- ◆ Use sequence, selection, and repetition in programs; work with variables and various forms of input and output.

Link back to computational thinking skills:

- ◆ Algorithmic thinking is the ability to think in terms of sequences and rules as a way of solving problems or understanding situations. It is a core skill that pupils develop when they learn to write their own computer programs.
- ◆ Formulating instructions to achieve a desired effect.
- ◆ Discuss errors and introduce the word debug, reflecting, problem solving, deduction.

Extending this activity – where next?

Put the coloured cards out in the wrong order for the character to cross the mat. Debug the instructions to get your character across the mat.

What is the shortest set of instructions needed to cross the mat from one side to the other?

Useful related online resources

BBC Bitesize – a short video clip explaining an algorithm:
https://www.bbc.com/bitesize/clips/z28qmp3

G = green Y = yellow
B = blue   R = red

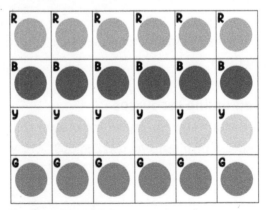

G = green Y = yellow
B = blue   R = red

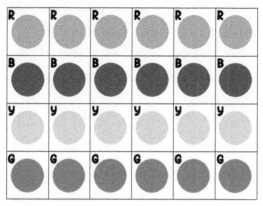

G = green   Y = yellow
B = blue   R = red

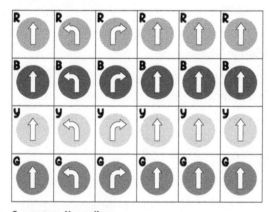

G = green   Y = yellow
B = blue   R = red

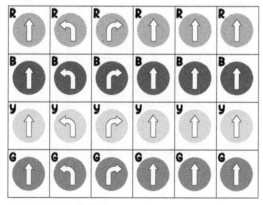

G = green   Y = yellow
B = blue   R = red

UNJUMBLE INSTRUCTIONS

Sorting out sequences of instructions, writing own instructions creating an algorithm

What you need:
◆ Printed sheets
◆ Pens
◆ Paper

Recommended age range:
Suitable for all ages

Prior knowledge/experience:
Your child will need to have completed Colour Sequence. They should also be familiar with the keyword 'algorithm'

What to do

Activity 1

Read through the instructions for sending a message on your mobile phone and put them in the right order. Write the correct numbers in order in the empty box below.

1. Turn phone on
2. Type the message
3. Pick up phone
4. Press send
5. Find message app
__ __ __ __ __

Activity 2

Now make a precise sequence of instructions for someone to switch on the television. Take care to sequence them in the right order. Use the table to write your instructions to switch on the TV.

Jumble up your instructions. Then see if someone can put them in the right order. Remember to talk about why you put your instructions in the order you chose.

Note: this activity may work better if one person writes the instructions and jumbles them up for another person to then try and rearrange them. Discussions about the placement of instructions will be key here for valuable learning opportunities.

What you're learning

This activity helps you learn about the importance of instructions. In programming, computers only follow exactly what they are told or programmed to do. So being able to think of a solution in clear and concise instructions is a valuable skill. Ask yourself questions such as 'What else do I need to do? Have I missed out any steps? What can I add to make the instructions work better?'

When completing Activity 2 make sure you follow the instructions precisely and only do what you are told. The sequence may need to be debugged for it to work correctly. If so, this is a valuable learning opportunity and one to be explored.

Link back to the National Curriculum for Computing:
Pupils should be taught to:
KS1

◆ Understand what algorithms are; how they are implemented as programs on digital devices; and that programs execute by following precise and unambiguous instructions.
◆ Create and debug simple programs.

KS2

◆ Design, write and debug programs that accomplish specific goals, including controlling or simulating physical systems; solve problems by decomposing them into smaller parts.
◆ Use sequence, selection, and repetition in programs; work with variables and various forms of input and output.

Link back to computational thinking skills:

◆ Formulating instructions to be followed in a given order (sequence).

Extending this activity – where next?
This activity could be developed further by coming up with different sequences that can be jumbled and unjumbled. For example, how to wash your hands or clean your teeth.

There are multiple coding and programming apps available on tablet devices. Try for example, Bee-Bot, A.L.E.X., Scratch Jr, Code Warriors, BlueBot and Lightbot amongst many others.

Useful related online resources

Barefoot Computing – a set of resources designed for schools to teach computing skills without using computers: https://www.barefootcomputing.org

Computer Science 4 Fun – a digital magazine presenting computer science concepts and research in easily digestible articles: http://www.cs4fn.org
Teaching London Computing – CS4N Doodle art Christmas activity: https://teachinglondoncomputing.org/algorithmic-doodle-art/

Creating a flowchart

What you need:

- ◆ Internet connection
- ◆ Pens
- ◆ Paper

Recommended age range:

Suitable for all ages

Prior knowledge/experience:

Need to have completed Colour Sequence and Unjumble Instructions

What to do

Watch this YouTube video:

https://www.youtube.com/watch?v=tBPRbXBjYrs

Note, other dance videos can also work. If you have the Just Dance game at home or watch the videos on the Just Dance YouTube channel, you'll be able to dance along easily and will find that the videos have a graphical algorithm on screen. These are known as Pictos, which are stick-figure diagrams that illustrate the dance move that needs to be made, in sequence.

What are the dance moves? Talk them through, can you explain them, describe them to someone else?

Let's break this dance down and work it out in steps. For very young children this may be a verbal discussion only, or written instructions may take the form of diagrams such as stick figures.

You may find it useful to use the flowchart structure below to help fill in the different dance steps in the sequence.

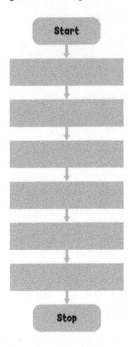

Now test the sequence out on someone else. Can they follow the instructions you've written in the sequence above to carry out the same dance routine?

If not, then what needs to be changed? Look through your algorithm to make the changes and improve the accuracy of your instructions.

Did you know you are testing and debugging your algorithm now?

Sometimes we can make instructions more accurate by adding more detail. Do you need to add any more detail? What's the clearest way to present this information?

Create your own dance move

Now that you know how to create an algorithm for an existing dance routine, can you work out how to create your own?

Make up your own dance move.

Write down the algorithm for it.

Test it on someone else. Can they follow the instructions accurately?

Get some feedback on what they thought. Ask them to fill in the scores and additional criteria below. Some blank rows have been left for you to complete. Perhaps you can come up with a few of your own success criteria as well.

Feedback Criteria

Score out of 4
(1 is low, 4 is high)

1. Clarity of instructions
2. Accuracy of the sequence
3. Use of words (concepts) such as repeat
4. Overall quality of the dance routine
5.
6.

What you're learning

This activity teaches you the need for precise and accurate wording in algorithms. It also covers how flowcharts can demonstrate dance sequences as an algorithm.

Link back to the National Curriculum for Computing:
Pupils should be taught to:
KS1

◆ Understand what algorithms are; how they are implemented as programs on digital devices; and that programs execute by following precise and unambiguous instructions.
◆ Create and debug simple programs.

KS2

- Design, write and debug programs that accomplish specific goals, including controlling or simulating physical systems; solve problems by decomposing them into smaller parts.
- Use sequence, selection, and repetition in programs; work with variables and various forms of input and output.

Link back to computational thinking skills:

- Algorithmic thinking through representing the dance sequences as an algorithm.
- Evaluation by reviewing your algorithm and continuing to improve it.
- Decomposition through breaking down the dance sequence into individual steps in order to write the algorithm.

Extending this activity– where next?

Create your own dance sequence. Combine some of your dance moves to create a dance routine. How often should a single move be repeated? What order should the moves take place in? Can you find an effective way to knit the algorithms together?

For a bit of fun watch the dance clip for The Haka on YouTube. Identify any repeating sequences – how can we represent this? Give the sequence a name and then write the name instead of having to write it out again.

Useful related online resources

Computer Science 4 Fun – a digital magazine presenting computer science concepts and research in easily digestible articles:

http://www.cs4fn.org

Digital Schoolhouse – the full Just Dance with the Algorithm activity, which builds upon the activity here (approximately 6 hours):

https://www.digitalschoolhouse.org.uk/workshop/just-dance-algorithm

THE COMPUTATIONAL DUCK

Using LEGO bricks to introduce algorithmic thinking

What you need:

◆ LEGO® bricks per child (for the main activity)
   ◆ 2 x 2x2 bricks (yellow)
   ◆ 1 x 2x4 bricks (yellow)
   ◆ 1 x 2x1 brick (yellow)
   ◆ 2 x 2x3 flat plate bricks (red)
◆ A range of additional bricks for the extension activity
◆ A digital alternative to LEGO bricks is the Virtual LEGO
   Builder (https://www.buildwithchrome.com/)

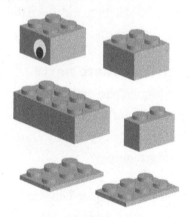

Recommended age range:
Suitable for all ages

Prior knowledge/experience:
Need to have completed Dancing Algorithms

What to do

Any combination of bricks can be used, but ensure that the child has
the two red and four yellow bricks to enable them to create their own

duck. Ask them to build a duck, but give them no further instructions. Encourage them to get creative, see what they develop; the child should independently create their own duck.

Note: if working with a single child then it will be useful if the grown-up can create their own version of the duck as well – this will aid comparison later.

After the duck has been created, compare your ducks. This is a good point for discussion as the ducks will be different. Ask 'why is each one different?' The answer is because of the instruction given. Simply saying 'Make a duck' leaves how a duck should look open to interpretation. As humans we add our own prior knowledge and make the duck according to how we think it should look. However, computers do not have that ability, they simply follow the algorithm programmed within them.

What you're learning

This activity uses a range of computational thinking techniques. The key skill developed here is algorithmic thinking, with children formulating their own instructions, that may be simply sequential or follow logical operations. Children work with their verbal instructions to create them in written form, which then may begin to see the introduction of programming concepts such as loops (also known as iteration). Loops are the concept of instructions being repeated several times. Rather than rewriting the same instructions again and again, we can simply tell the computer to repeat them a given number of times or until a particular condition has been met.

Link back to the National Curriculum for Computing:

Pupils should be taught to:

KS1

- ◆ Understand what algorithms are; how they are implemented as programs on digital devices; and that programs execute by following precise and unambiguous instructions.

◆ Create and debug simple programs.

KS2

◆ Design, write and debug programs that accomplish specific goals, including controlling or simulating physical systems; solve problems by decomposing them into smaller parts.

◆ Use sequence, selection, and repetition in programs; work with variables and various forms of input and output.

Link back to computational thinking skills:

◆ Algorithmic thinking through following and providing the instructions to create a duck out of LEGO.

◆ Evaluation by reviewing your algorithm and continuing to improve it.

◆ Decomposition through breaking the duck down into its constituent parts in order to be able to develop an algorithm.

Extending this activity- where next?

There are a range of activities that can be carried out using different coloured bricks. The activity carried out can be easily extended, with children developing their own versions. Try this:

Ask your child to pick six of their own bricks and then:

◆ Use them to create an object, such as a tree
◆ Develop an algorithm for the object
◆ Give the bricks (without the algorithm) to another person
◆ Is the object they create identical to yours?
◆ Now try it with the algorithm? Does it work?

This is an extended set of shorter activities that builds upon the previous activity, 'The Computational Duck', and allows children to explore and compare algorithms in different formats, introducing the concept of evaluation. *Please note: if short on time you may not want to work your way through all the activities in one sitting. Also, be aware that when working your way through these, it is worth doing them in order as they progress in difficulty level.*

What you need:

◆ At least six LEGO® bricks per child (for the main activity)

Recommended age range:

Suitable for age seven upwards

Prior knowledge/experience:

Should have had a basic introduction to algorithms and have completed The Computational Duck activity

What to do

The activity encourages children to examine algorithms in different forms.

This works best in pairs. There are two distinct roles for the children to play, and both will take it in turns to play each role. One child will play the role of the 'programmer' and the other will be the 'human computer'. It will be the job of the programmer to describe their duck to the computer.

Verbal Instructions Round

Instruct the child to give their partner verbal instructions to recreate their duck. It is worth noting that this activity can be repeated several times with different levels of questioning attached to each. For example:

- Round 1 – free discussion between the pair, no restrictions
- Round 2 – allow the (child) computer to give feedback on whether or not they understood the instruction, but not ask any questions
- Round 3 – the (child) computer gives no feedback on the instruction, they simply execute the instruction given as best as they can

Engage children in a discussion about the algorithms they gave their partner:

- How successful was their algorithm?
- Did they have to refine their algorithm at all?
- How easy was it to describe their duck in a way that enabled their partner to recreate it?
- As the children worked through the rounds did the process become easier or more difficult?

Rounds 2 and 3 begin to illustrate the importance of computer feedback and systems with well-designed error messages. What type of response from the (child) computer was the most helpful? Why?

Written Instructions Round

Ask the child to write down the algorithm that would enable their partner to create the exact duck model that they have made.

Ask the children to swap instructions. Each child should test the instructions of their partner; are they able to recreate the same duck? Engage children in a discussion about what they have found. Some starting points may be:

- Give an example of a very good instruction – what made this a good instruction?
- Give an example of an instruction that was difficult to follow – why was this difficult?
- How long did it take to follow the algorithm?
- Were the instructions accurate?

Graphical Instructions Round

When LEGO issue building instructions for their kits, the algorithms are graphical rather than text-based. Why? Ask the children to examine existing LEGO building instructions (if you do not have any around the home then examples are available online at https://wwwsecure.us.lego.com/en-gb/service/buildinginstructions).

- What is common about each set of building instructions?
- What are the differences between each instruction set?
- Why are they easy to follow?

Engage children in a discussion about the importance of good algorithms. What have they learned from the tasks they have carried out so far?

Ask the children to draw their own building instructions for their duck and then test them on their partner. Use discussion to help draw out the key elements of the activity and what makes the graphical representation of the algorithm so effective for the duck-building exercise.

Evaluating Algorithms

Think about the different algorithms that have been developed for the duck.

- Are the algorithms better written out or drawn?
- What difference does it make?

- Why?
- Which algorithm was easier to produce?
- Which algorithm was easier to follow?

If you want to take a more formal approach to the evaluation of the different algorithms you can work with the children to devise a set of evaluation criteria that they can then test. These criteria could include:

- The speed of the algorithm: how long did it take to give out all the instructions? Was the algorithm overly complicated or could it have been simplified?
- The length of time it took to create the duck by following each algorithm
- The efficiency of the algorithm
- Was the end result accurate?
- How many errors were made by following the algorithm?
- How easy was the algorithm to follow?

You may want to take one element and think of how that could be tested. How would you know whether you have met each criterion or not?

What you're learning

This activity uses a range of computational thinking techniques. The key skill developed here is algorithmic thinking, with children formulating their own instructions, that may be simply sequential or follow logical operations. Children work with their verbal instructions to create them in written form, which then may begin to see the introduction of programming concepts such as loops (iteration).

The construction of the duck enables the children to touch upon abstraction and decomposition. For example, they need to be able to identify the different parts of the duck that can be represented through the six bricks. While this in itself is decomposition, abstraction enables them to realise that they will not create an exact replica of the duck. Key details about the features of a duck will need to be ignored if they are going to create their own model replica using only six LEGO bricks. Adults can engage in discussion to help children see what details they automatically began to ignore about ducks.

Continuous evaluation enables students to constantly test and debug their algorithms. Key discussions around the effectiveness of different algorithms enable them to see if it is fit for purpose. Were there alternative solutions, what did their peers come up with? These are all valuable considerations and it is important, if possible, to enable children to try and arrive at their own evaluation criterion.

Extending this activity – where next?

Did you enjoy this activity? This work has been developed with inspiration from the work of the LEGO Foundation and the six bricks project. Find out more about the project and download further activities and classroom resources from the LEGO Foundation website.[4]

The six bricks booklet sets out a number of activities to help children develop their problem-solving, memory, creativity and movement skills. Many of these activities also serve as excellent ideas to help develop computational thinking and, delivered appropriately with the correct emphasis, they will work for children of varying ages and abilities. These activities include:

Back-to-Back

◆ Two children stand back-to-back with the same three bricks

4 http://www.legofoundation.com/es-es/programmes/play-based-learning/six-bricks

- One child builds a model and then explains to their partner how to build the same model
- The partner builds without looking or asking questions
- The pair compare models and discuss how it went

The activity strongly emphasises algorithmic thinking and evaluation skills.

What Can You Build?
- Your child uses six bricks to build any creature
- They then describe their creature

This simple activity helps develop a child's creativity and can fit in with any theme or subject. There is some opportunity to consider abstraction here.

Build a Cube
- Build a cube with six bricks

This is a logical puzzle that will require logical reasoning to solve the problem. Your child will constantly evaluate their outcome and the activity can be extended to see:

- How fast can they do it?
- Can they write an algorithm to create the cube?

For more information about LEGO Education visit
www.LEGOEducation.co.uk

CHAPTER 4

Data Representation

LEGO BRICK BINARY PLACE VALUE

Learn how computers represent numbers, using LEGO bricks
to help you

What you need:

◆ 1 x 2x4 LEGO brick

◆ 1 x 2x2 LEGO brick

◆ 1 x 2x1 LEGO brick

◆ 1 stud LEGO brick

◆ Baseplate (optional)

Recommended age range:
Suitable for all ages

Prior knowledge/experience:
None

What to do

Lay out your LEGO bricks in descending height order, like so:

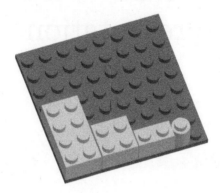

The order is important, you should have the 2x4 (eight-stud brick) on the far left, then the 2x2 (four studs), then the 2x1 (two studs) and finally the 1 (one stud).

You should then count the total number of studs to work out what number is being represented. In this example there are fifteen in total so the number being represented is fifteen.

If the brick is present it will be represented by a one and if it is not there by a zero. This means that the binary for the number fifteen would be 1111 as all of the bricks are needed to make a total of fifteen studs.

Let's take some of the bricks away.

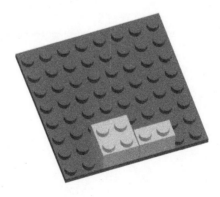

I have taken the bricks from the right- and left-hand side of the base-plate so my binary number now looks like this: 0110.

What number is being represented now? Count the studs. There are six.

Now try the worksheet at the end of this activity!

What you're learning

The activity explains how binary place value works; just like in decimal the place value of the number on the far right is always 1 and, unlike decimal, each new additional place value added to the left of this number is double the previous place value; 1 then 2, then 4 and then 8 but in this order: 8421.

A 1 or 0 is then used to represent whether to include that place value in the total or not. 1111 means add all the place values together which equals fifteen. 1010 means add eight and two to equal ten.

Link back to the National Curriculum for Computing:

◆ Design, use and evaluate computational abstractions that model the state and behaviour of real-world problems and physical systems.
◆ Understand how data of various types (including text, sounds and pictures) can be represented and manipulated digitally, in the form of binary digits.
◆ Understand how numbers can be represented in binary, and be able to carry out simple operations on binary numbers [for example, binary addition, and conversion between binary and decimal].

Link back to computational thinking skills:

- ◆ Formulating instructions to achieve a desired effect.
- ◆ Formulating instructions to be followed in a given order (sequence).
- ◆ Formulating instructions that use arithmetic and logical operations.
- ◆ Writing sequences of instructions that store, move and manipulate data (variables and assignment).
- ◆ Writing instructions that choose between different constituent instructions (selection).
- ◆ Writing instructions that repeat groups of constituent instructions (loops/iteration).
- ◆ Breaking down artefacts into constituent parts to make them easier to work with.
- ◆ Breaking down a problem into simpler versions of the same problem that can be solved in the same way.
- ◆ Identifying patterns and commonalities in artefacts.

Extending this activity- where next?

Try the following activities:

- ◆ Binary Light Switches p.52
- ◆ Binary Playing Cards p.55

Worksheets

Binary	Decimal
0000	
0001	
0010	
0011	
0100	
0101	
0110	

0111	
1000	
1001	
1010	
1011	
1100	
1101	
1110	
1111	

Answers to Worksheets

Binary	Decimal
0000	0
0001	1
0010	2
0011	3
0100	4
0101	5
0110	6
0111	7
1000	8
1001	9
1010	10
1011	11
1100	12
1101	13
1110	14
1111	15

BINARY LIGHT SWITCHES

Find out how binary is represented using light switches

What you need:
- ◆ Bank of light switches
- ◆ As an alternative, four items with switches on them, such as a hair dryer, kettle, electric toothbrush, torch, etc.

Recommended age range:
Suitable for all ages

Prior knowledge/experience:
Your child should have completed the LEGO Brick Binary Place Values activity

What to do

Use a set of light switches to represent a binary number:

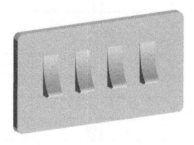

Remember the place values double each time starting from one on the right.

If the light switch is on it is represented with a one and if it is off a zero.

The switches above would represent 0000 and the number zero.

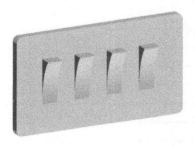

In this image all the switches are on so the binary number would be 1111 and the decimal value fifteen.

Now have a go at the worksheet.

What you're learning

Computers represent everything as binary numbers. The reason for this is that computers are made up of millions of transistors which work like switches. This activity demonstrates how the binary numbers actually relate to each switch and the decimal number it represents.

Link back to the National Curriculum for Computing:
KS3

- ◆ Design, use and evaluate computational abstractions that model the state and behaviour of real-world problems and physical systems:
  - ○ understand simple Boolean logic (for example, AND, OR and NOT) and some of its uses in circuits and programming
  - ○ understand how data of various types (including text, sounds and pictures) can be represented and manipulated digitally, in the form of binary digits
  - ○ understand how numbers can be represented in binary, and be able to carry out simple operations on binary numbers (for example, binary addition and conversion between binary and decimal)

Worksheets

Binary	Decimal
	0
	1
	2
	3
	4
	5
	6
	7
	8
	9
	10
	11
	12
	13
	14
	15

Activity Answers

Binary	Decimal
0000	0
0001	1
0010	2
0011	3
0100	4
0101	5
0110	6
0111	7
1000	8
1001	9
1010	10
1011	11
1100	12
1101	13
1110	14
1111	15

BINARY PLAYING CARDS

Find out how to represent binary numbers using playing cards
  What you need:
  ◆ Playing cards

Recommended age range:
Suitable for all ages

Prior knowledge/experience:
Your child should have completed the LEGO Brick Binary Place
Values activity

What to do

Take the following playing cards, from any suit, from a standard deck
of cards: an Ace, two, four and eight.

In this example the Ace will be equal to one.

Lay out the cards face up on the placeholder worksheet:

Where the card is face up it represents a 1 in the binary number and
you should include the number on the card when adding the place
values together. A face-down card represents a 0 in the binary number.

These cards represent the following binary number: 1111. The decimal number they represent is 15 (8 + 4 + 2 + 1 = 15).

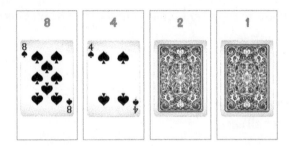

The binary number represented here is 1100 and the decimal number 12 (8 + 4 = 12).

Now try the combinations below. Can you work out what decimal number each binary string represents?

Binary	Decimal
0000	
0001	
0010	
0011	
0100	
0101	
0110	
0111	
1000	
1001	
1010	
1011	
1100	
1101	
1110	
1111	

What you're learning

The activity explains how binary place value works. Just like in decimal, the place value of the number on the far right is always 1. Unlike decimal, each new additional place value added to the left of this number is double the previous place value: 1 then 2, then 4 and then 8, but in this order: 8421.

A 1 or 0 is then used to represent whether to include that place value in the total or not.

1111 means add all the place values together to equal 15.

1010 means add 8 and 2 to equal 10.

Link back to the National Curriculum for Computing:
- Design, use and evaluate computational abstractions that model the state and behaviour of real-world problems and physical systems.
- Understand how data of various types (including text, sounds and pictures) can be represented and manipulated digitally, in the form of binary digits.
- Understand how numbers can be represented in binary, and be able to carry out simple operations on binary numbers [for example, binary addition, and conversion between binary and decimal].

Link back to computational thinking skills:
- Formulating instructions to achieve a desired effect.
- Formulating instructions to be followed in a given order (sequence).
- Formulating instructions that use arithmetic and logical operations.
- Writing sequences of instructions that store, move and manipulate data (variables and assignment).
- Writing instructions that choose between different constituent instructions (selection).

- Writing instructions that repeat groups of constituent instructions (loops/iteration).
- Breaking down artefacts into constituent parts to make them easier to work with.
- Breaking down a problem into simpler versions of the same problem that can be solved in the same way.
- Identifying patterns and commonalities in artefacts.

Extending this activity – where next?

Did you know that individual binary digits (also known as bits) are usually grouped together? A collection of four binary digits (or four bits) is referred to as a 'nibble' and a collection of eight bits is referred to as a byte. When we measure computer memory we often do this by counting the number of bytes being used.

Using the internet as a resource, can you find out how many bytes are in a:

- Kilobyte
- Megabyte
- Gigabyte
- Terabyte

What if you used five bits instead of four? What is the maximum value that you can make with that? The more bits that you use, the more values that can be held, which means the more data a computer can store.

Computers commonly use 'bytes', which is a collection of eight bits. Use additional playing cards to create spaces for eight bits and see if you can work out the following:

1) What is the value of the highest bit (i.e. the one furthest to the left)?

2) Using eight bits what is the highest number that can be created?

3) What is the maximum number of combinations that can be created with eight bits? *Hint: zero counts*

Answers

3) 256

2) 255

1) 128

Useful related online resources

Paint by Pixels – based on paint by numbers this activity helps students understand the concept of binary digits: https://www.digitalschoolhouse.org.uk/documents/paint-pixels

CS4FN – Puzzle book:
   https://teachinglondoncomputing.org/puzzle-book-1/
Maths Is Fun – Binary Digits:
   https://www.mathsisfun.com/binary-digits.html

Activity Answers

Binary	Decimal
0000	0
0001	1
0010	2
0011	3
0100	4
0101	5
0110	6
0111	7
1000	8
1001	9
1010	10

1011	11
1100	12
1101	13
1110	14
1111	15

Worksheets

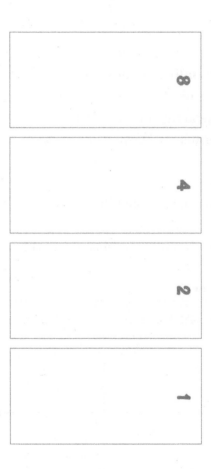

What to do

Place each of your bottles on a coaster like this:

Each coaster has a value:

$$\underline{8} \quad \underline{4} \quad \underline{2} \quad \underline{1}$$

If a coaster is empty then it has no value.

If a coaster has a bottle on it, we can use the value as explained above.

So, this diagram illustrates the value: 8 + 4 + 2 + 1 = 15

This is 1:

__ __ __ █

This is 2:

__ __ █ __

This is 3:

__ __ █ █

And so on.

Sing the song 'Ten Green Bottles', moving the bottles to represent the number in each verse in binary:

Ten green bottles sitting on the wall,	🍾	🍾
Ten green bottles sitting on the wall,	🍾	🍾
And if one green bottle should accidentally fall,	🍾	🍾 →
There'll be nine green bottles sitting on the wall.	🍾	🍾

See the worksheet for the full lyrics for 'Ten Green Bottles'

What you're learning

The activity explains how binary place value works. Just like in decimal, the place value of the number on the far right is always 1. Unlike decimal, each new additional place value added to the left of this number is double the previous place value: 1 then 2, then 4 and then 8 but in this order – 8421.

A 1 or 0 is then used to represent whether to include that place value in the total or not.

1111 means add all the place values together to equal 15.

1010 means add 8 and 2 to equal 10.

Link back to the National Curriculum for Computing:

- ◆ Design, use and evaluate computational abstractions that model the state and behaviour of real-world problems and physical systems.
- ◆ Understand how data of various types (including text, sounds and pictures) can be represented and manipulated digitally, in the form of binary digits.
- ◆ Understand how numbers can be represented in binary, and be able to carry out simple operations on binary numbers (for example, binary addition, and conversion between binary and decimal).

Link back to computational thinking skills:

- ◆ Formulating instructions to achieve a desired effect.
- ◆ Formulating instructions to be followed in a given order (sequence).
- ◆ Formulating instructions that use arithmetic and logical operations.

- Writing sequences of instructions that store, move and manipulate data (variables and assignment).
- Writing instructions that choose between different constituent instructions (selection).
- Writing instructions that repeat groups of constituent instructions (loops/iteration).
- Breaking down artefacts into constituent parts to make them easier to work with.
- Breaking down a problem into simpler versions of the same problem that can be solved in the same way.
- Identifying patterns and commonalities in artefacts.

Worksheet

Ten green bottles sitting on the wall,
Ten green bottles sitting on the wall,
And if one green bottle should accidentally fall,
There'll be nine green bottles sitting on the wall.

Nine green bottles sitting on the wall,
Nine green bottles sitting on the wall,
And if one green bottle should accidentally fall,
There'll be eight green bottles sitting on the wall.

Eight green bottles sitting on the wall,
Eight green bottles sitting on the wall,
And if one green bottle should accidentally fall,
There'll be seven green bottles sitting on the wall.

Seven green bottles sitting on the wall,
Seven green bottles sitting on the wall,
And if one green bottle should accidentally fall,
There'll be six green bottles sitting on the wall.

Six green bottles sitting on the wall,
Six green bottles sitting on the wall,
And if one green bottle should accidentally fall,
There'll be five green bottles sitting on the wall.

Five green bottles sitting on the wall,
Five green bottles sitting on the wall,
And if one green bottle should accidentally fall,
There'll be four green bottles sitting on the wall.

Four green bottles sitting on the wall,
Four green bottles sitting on the wall,
And if one green bottle should accidentally fall,
There'll be three green bottles sitting on the wall.

Three green bottles sitting on the wall,
Three green bottles sitting on the wall,
And if one green bottle should accidentally fall,
There'll be two green bottles sitting on the wall.

Two green bottles sitting on the wall,
Two green bottles sitting on the wall,
And if one green bottle should accidentally fall,
There'll be one green bottle sitting on the wall.

One green bottle sitting on the wall,
One green bottle sitting on the wall,
And if one green bottle should accidentally fall,
There'll be zero green bottles sitting on the wall.

Worksheet answers

Ten green bottles sitting on the wall,		
Ten green bottles sitting on the wall,		
And if one green bottle should accidentally fall,		
There'll be nine green bottles sitting on the wall.		

Nine green bottles sitting on the wall,		
Nine green bottles sitting on the wall,		
And if one green bottle should accidentally fall,		
There'll be eight green bottles sitting on the wall.		

Eight green bottles sitting on the wall,	
Eight green bottles sitting on the wall,	
And if one green bottle should accidentally fall,	
There'll be seven green bottles sitting on the wall.	

Seven green bottles sitting on the wall,	
Seven green bottles sitting on the wall,	
And if one green bottle should accidentally fall,	
There'll be six green bottles sitting on the wall.	

Six green bottles sitting on the wall,	
Six green bottles sitting on the wall,	
And if one green bottle should accidentally fall,	
There'll be five green bottles sitting on the wall.	

Five green bottles sitting on the wall,	
Five green bottles sitting on the wall,	
And if one green bottle should accidentally fall,	
There'll be four green bottles sitting on the wall.	

Four green bottles sitting on the wall,	
Four green bottles sitting on the wall,	
And if one green bottle should accidentally fall,	
There'll be three green bottles sitting on the wall.	

Three green bottles sitting on the wall,	
Three green bottles sitting on the wall,	
And if one green bottle should accidentally fall,	
There'll be two green bottles sitting on the wall.	

Two green bottles sitting on the wall,	
Two green bottles sitting on the wall,	
And if one green bottle should accidentally fall,	
There'll be one green bottle sitting on the wall.	

One green bottle sitting on the wall,	
One green bottle sitting on the wall,	
And if one green bottle should accidentally fall,	
There'll be zero green bottles sitting on the wall.	

Extending this activity – where next?

Rhymes and stories can often help us understand concepts. Think of other nursery rhymes or songs that you know. Could any of them be adapted in this way to illustrate binary concepts? For example, what about the song 'Ten in the Bed'?

Useful related online resources

Paint by Pixels – based on paint by numbers this activity helps students understand the concept of binary digits: https://www.digitalschoolhouse.org.uk/documents/paint-pixels

CS4FN – Puzzle book: https://teachinglondoncomputing.org/puzzle-book-1/

A BINARY STORY

Use your binary number representation skills to save the village
   What you need:
   ◆ Four candles, tea lights or torches
   ◆ A lighter or matches (if using candles or tea lights)

Recommended age range:
Suitable for all ages

Prior knowledge/experience:
Your child should have completed the LEGO Brick Binary Place Values, Binary Light Switches and Binary Playing Cards activities

---

What to do

Lay out your candles like so:

Now tell the story:

Once upon a time in Arvok, which is famous for its strawberries, villages were plagued by bandits. The villagers were getting fed up with the bandits stealing their grain, apples and strawberries. The king of the land was reluctant to send out all his troops every time a village was being attacked. He also didn't want all his troops camped out at villages waiting for the bandits to plunder, so he devised a plan to work out how many bandits were attacking his villages so he could send out twice as many troops to capture them. He needed a way for the villagers to let him know how many bandits were attacking their village, so he consulted his mathematician.

The mathematician suggested that the villagers light a beacon to indicate they were being attacked. 'But how would I know how many bandits there are?' the king asked, 'and how many troops to send?'

'Ah,' said the mathematician, 'we can use binary. If we have four fires, we can count up to fifteen and the villagers will be able to tell us how many bandits are attacking them.'

Now complete the worksheet. For the best impact, light the candles or torches to represent the beacons in each line of the worksheet:

Points for discussion

How can the villagers use the four beacons to tell the King how many troops they need? Think about the different options. Suggest binary as a prompt if your child hasn't done so already. How can you use the beacons to represent numbers up to fifteen in binary?

The same binary system can be used to represent significantly larger numbers, as each place value will double. So, for example, if you were to use eight beacons, then the highest number you could represent would be 255:

$$128 + 64 + 32 + 16 + 8 + 4 + 2 + 1 = 255$$

How could the villagers let the King know that there were more than fifteen bandits? Discuss how numbers up to 255 can be represented with eight beacons.

What you're learning

The activity explains how binary place value works. Just like in decimal, the place value of the number on the far right is always 1. Unlike decimal, each new additional place value added to the left of this number is double the previous place value: 1 then 2, then 4 and then 8, but in this order: 8421.

1 or 0 is then used to represent whether to include that place value in the total or not.

1111 means add all the place values together to equal 15.

1010 means add 8 and 2 to equal 10.

Link back to the National Curriculum for Computing:

◆ Design, use and evaluate computational abstractions that model the state and behaviour of real-world problems and physical systems.

- Understand how data of various types (including text, sounds and pictures) can be represented and manipulated digitally, in the form of binary digits.
- Understand how numbers can be represented in binary, and be able to carry out simple operations on binary numbers (for example, binary addition, and conversion between binary and decimal).

Link back to computational thinking skills:
- Formulating instructions to achieve a desired effect.
- Formulating instructions to be followed in a given order (sequence).
- Formulating instructions that use arithmetic and logical operations.
- Writing sequences of instructions that store, move and manipulate data (variables and assignment).
- Writing instructions that choose between different constituent instructions (selection).
- Writing instructions that repeat groups of constituent instructions (loops/iteration).
- Breaking down artefacts into constituent parts to make them easier to work with.
- Breaking down a problem into simpler versions of the same problem that can be solved in the same way.
- Identifying patterns and commonalities in artefacts.

Worksheets
Complete the table. Where there are blanks in the grid either add a 1 or 0 to show if the beacon is on or off.

8	4	2	1		
					0
				=	
					10
					8
					1
					6

Worksheet answers

8	4	2	1		=
unlit torch	unlit torch	unlit torch	unlit torch		0
lit torch	unlit torch	lit torch	lit torch		11
unlit torch	lit torch	unlit torch	lit torch		5
unlit torch	lit torch	lit torch	lit torch		7
lit torch	lit torch	lit torch	unlit torch		14
unlit torch	0	lit torch	lit torch		3
lit torch	lit torch	lit torch	lit torch		15
1	unlit torch	1	unlit torch		10
lit torch	0	0	0		8
0	0	0	lit torch		1
unlit torch	1	1	0		6

Useful related online resources

BBC Bitesize – Find out more about binary and how it's used in the world around us:

https://www.bbc.co.uk/bitesize/guides/z26rcdm/revision/1

BINARY SHIFT PLAYING CARDS

Find out how to multiply numbers using a binary shift using playing cards.

What you need:
- ◆ Playing cards

Recommended age range:
Suitable for all ages

Prior knowledge/experience:
Your child should have completed the LEGO Brick Binary Place Values and Binary Playing Cards activities

---

What to do

Take the following playing cards from any suit in a standard pack of playing cards: an Ace, two, four and eight.

In this example Ace will be equal to one.

Lay out the cards to represent a binary number leaving the place value 8 column empty:

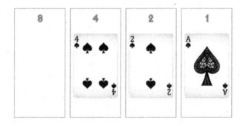

As before, the cards that are face up are included in the sum. So, in this case, you are representing the number 7 (4 + 2 + 1 = 7).

Move the cards one place to the left into the 8 column and backfill the empty 1 with a facedown card:

Replace each of the face-up cards with the card that represents the correct place value:

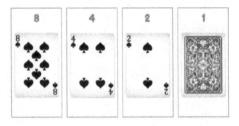

Now work out the new number (8 + 4 + 2 = 14).
You have just multiplied the first number by two!

Now see if you can work out the answers to the problems below:

Binary	Decimal Value	Shift	New Binary Value	New Decimal Value
0001		one place to left		
0010		one place to left		
0011		one place to left		
0100		one place to left		
0101		one place to left		
0110		one place to left		

0111		one place to left		
0001		two places to left		
0010		two places to left		
0011		two places to left		
0100		two places to left		
0101		two places to left		
0110		two places to left		
0111		two places to left		

What you're learning

The activity explains how binary shift works. A shift to the left of one place multiplies the original number by two. Shifting two places to the left will multiply the original number by four.

Link back to the National Curriculum for Computing:

◆ Design, use and evaluate computational abstractions that model the state and behaviour of real-world problems and physical systems.

◆ Understand how data of various types (including text, sounds and pictures) can be represented and manipulated digitally, in the form of binary digits.

◆ Understand how numbers can be represented in binary, and be able to carry out simple operations on binary numbers (for example, binary addition, and conversion between binary and decimal).

Link back to computational thinking skills:

◆ Formulating instructions to achieve a desired effect.

◆ Formulating instructions to be followed in a given order (sequence).

◆ Formulating instructions that use arithmetic and logical operations.

◆ Writing sequences of instructions that store, move and manipulate data (variables and assignment).

- Writing instructions that choose between different constituent instructions (selection).
- Writing instructions that repeat groups of constituent instructions (loops/iteration).
- Breaking down artefacts into constituent parts to make them easier to work with.
- Breaking down a problem into simpler versions of the same problem that can be solved in the same way.
- Identifying patterns and commonalities in artefacts.

Extending this activity - where next?

You can perform a shift to the right to divide numbers too. Lay the cards out like this:

As before, the cards that are face up are included in the sum and cards that are face down are not. So, in this case you are representing the number 10 (8 + 2 = 10).

Move the cards one place to the right, discarding what is currently in the 1 column and backfilling the empty 8 column with a face-down card:

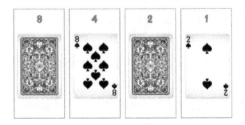

Replace each of the face-up cards with the card that represents the correct place value:

Now work out the new number (4 + 1 = 5).

You have just divided the first number by 2.

There is a little more to it with dividing as you have to handle decimal numbers (which is outside the remit of this book).

Answers

Binary	Decimal Value	Shift	New Binary Value	New Decimal Value
0001	1	one place to left	0010	2
0010	2	one place to left	0100	4
0011	3	one place to left	0110	6
0100	4	one place to left	1000	8
0101	5	one place to left	1010	10
0110	6	one place to left	1100	12
0111	7	one place to left	1110	14
0001	1	two places to left	0100	4
0010	2	two places to left	1000	8
0011	3	two places to left	1100	12
0100	4	two places to left	10000	16
0101	5	two places to left	10100	20
0110	6	two places to left	11000	24
0111	7	two places to left	11100	28

Worksheets

THE MIND BOGGLES: BOGGLE PICTURES!

Understand how image representation works using Boggle

What you need:

◆ Boggle game set or enough dice to create a grid (Boggle uses 16 dice)

◆ Alternatively use the blank Boggle grid in the worksheet section

◆ Paper

◆ Coloured pencils, crayons or felt tips

Recommended age range:

Suitable for all ages

Prior knowledge/experience:

Previous data representation activities

What to do

Randomly place letters into the Boggle grid:

A	D	Z	M
R	G	Y	D
S	C	E	D
S	W	X	A

Using the colour allocation worksheet, allocate a colour to each letter:

A	Red	N	
B		O	
C		P	
D	Yellow	Q	
E		R	

F		S	
G		T	
H		U	
I		V	
J		W	
K		X	
L		Y	
M	Purple	Z	Blue

Using the blank grid, colour in the squares as instructed by the Boggle dice:

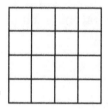

What you're learning

In order to represent more colours you would need more options on your dice to allocate the colours to. Computers do this by using longer binary numbers which allow them to have more number combinations and therefore represent more colours.

You now have twenty-six possible colours as there are twenty-six letters in the alphabet.

Link back to the National Curriculum for Computing:
 ◆ Understand how data of various types (including text, sounds and pictures) can be represented and manipulated digitally, in the form of binary digits.

Link back to computational thinking skills:
 ◆ Formulating instructions to achieve a desired effect.
 ◆ Breaking down artefacts into constituent parts to make them easier to work with.
 ◆ Identifying patterns and commonalities in artefacts.

Worksheets

Colour allocations

A		N	
B		O	
C		P	
D		Q	
E		R	
F		S	
G		T	
H		U	
I		V	
J		W	
K		X	
L		Y	
M		Z	

Blank colouring grid

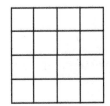

Blank Boggle grid

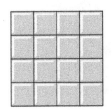

Extending this activity - where next?

Try adapting the grid – explore grids of different shapes and sizes. You might want to create a bookmark for example. Or how about encoding your name in different colours? Can you replace the coloured grid with beads and make a bracelet? Try the activity 'Hama Bead ASCII' below.

Useful related online resources

Paint by Pixels – based on paint by numbers this activity helps students understand the concept of binary digits:

https://www.digitalschoolhouse.org.uk/documents/paint-pixels

CS4FN – Puzzle book:

https://teachinglondoncomputing.org/puzzle-book-1/

HAMA BEAD ASCII

Represent your name in Hama beads using binary and ASCII code

What you need:
◆ Hama beads
◆ Hama bead pegboard template with a width of at least seven pegs
◆ Iron
◆ Baking paper
◆ Paper
◆ Pen

Recommended age range:
Suitable for all ages (care will need to be taken with ironing the Hama beads if working with younger children)

Prior knowledge/experience:
Your child should have completed the LEGO Brick Binary Place
Values, Binary Light Switches and Binary Playing Cards
activities

What to do

Write out your name leaving space after each letter. To keep things
simple let's use capital letters only. For example:

D

I

G

I

T

A

L

Look up the binary value of each of your letters:

Decimal	Binary	ASCII Character
65	01000001	A
66	01000010	B
67	01000011	C
68	01000100	D
69	01000101	E
70	01000110	F
71	01000111	G
72	01001000	H
73	01001001	I
74	01001010	J
75	01001011	K
76	01001100	L
77	01001101	M

78	01001110	N
79	01001111	O
80	01010000	P
81	01010001	Q
82	01010010	R
83	01010011	S
84	01010100	T
85	01010101	U
86	01010110	V
87	01010111	W
88	01011000	X
89	01011001	Y
90	01011010	Z

For example:

D	01000100
I	01001001
G	01000111
I	01001001
T	01010100
A	01000001
L	01001100

Now choose two colours of Hama bead, one to represent 1s and one for 0s.

I am going to use white to represent 1s and black for 0s.

Place the Hama beads onto your pegboard according to the binary number for each letter.

Here I have laid out the Hama beads to represent the binary number 01000100 which represents the letter D in ASCII:

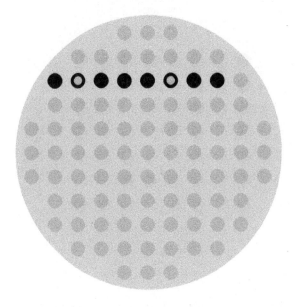

Add the rest of the Hama beads needed to represent your name:

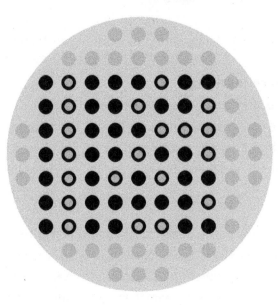

Fill in the rest of the space on your pegboard with a third colour:

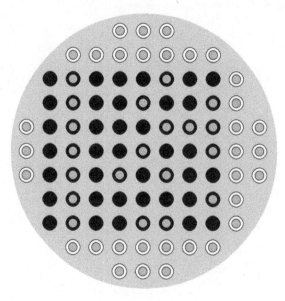

Cover your completed pegboard with the baking paper and then iron to melt the Hama beads together.

You have created a coaster with your name in ASCII and binary.

What you're learning

As we have previously discussed, everything on a computer is represented using binary, including letters. In computer science we call everything that you can type on a keyboard a character; this includes letters, numbers, symbols and control keys like enter and tab.

In the early sixties the American Standard Code for Information Interchange (ASCII) was developed in order to provide a standard character set for computers and electronic devices. Until then different companies used different character sets in their devices and so computers from different manufacturers were unable to communicate with each other as the binary number 01000100 might be a D on one computer but A on another.

ASCII uses 7 bits to represent 128 characters with an 8th bit being used as a check to make sure the binary number is correct (this is always a 0).

Link back to the National Curriculum for Computing:
◆ Design, use and evaluate computational abstractions that model the state and behaviour of real-world problems and physical systems.
◆ Understand how numbers can be represented in binary.
◆ Understand the hardware and software components that make up computer systems, and how they communicate with one another and with other systems.
◆ Understand how instructions are stored and executed within a computer system; understand how data of various types (including text, sounds and pictures) can be represented and manipulated digitally, in the form of binary digits.

Link back to computational thinking skills:
◆ Formulating instructions to achieve a desired effect.
◆ Formulating instructions to be followed in a given order (sequence).
◆ Breaking down artefacts into constituent parts to make them easier to work with.
◆ Identifying patterns and commonalities in artefacts.
◆ Adapting solutions, or parts of solutions, so they apply to a whole class of similar problems.
◆ Transferring ideas and solutions from one problem area to another.
◆ Choosing a way to represent an artefact, to allow it to be manipulated in useful ways.

Extending this activity – where next?

Can you think of other names you want to represent? Perhaps you could make several coasters, each one representing a separate word so that when you put them together they make a special encoded sentence.

Useful related online resources

Paint by Pixels – based on paint by numbers this activity helps students understand the concept of binary digits:

https://www.digitalschoolhouse.org.uk/documents/paint-pixels

CS4FN – Puzzle book:

https://teachinglondoncomputing.org/puzzle-book-1/

BRACELET ASCII

Represent your initials on a bracelet using binary and ASCII code

What you need:
- ◆ Beads
- ◆ String or cord
- ◆ Paper
- ◆ Pen

Recommended age range:
Suitable for all ages

Prior knowledge/experience:
Your child should have completed the LEGO Brick Binary Place Values, Binary Light Switches, Binary Playing Cards, The Mind Boggles: Boggle Pictures! and Hama Bead ASCII activities

What to do

Write out your initials leaving space after each letter; to keep things simple let's use capital letters only. For example:

D

S

H

Look up the ASCII value of each of your letters:

Decimal	Binary	ASCII Character
65	01000001	A
66	01000010	B
67	01000011	C
68	01000100	D
69	01000101	E
70	01000110	F
71	01000111	G
72	01001000	H
73	01001001	I
74	01001010	J
75	01001011	K
76	01001100	L
77	01001101	M
78	01001110	N
79	01001111	O
80	01010000	P
81	01010001	Q
82	01010010	R
83	01010011	S
84	01010100	T
85	01010101	U
86	01010110	V
87	01010111	W
88	01011000	X
89	01011001	Y
90	01011010	Z

D	01000100
S	01010011
H	01001000

Now choose two colours of beads, one to represent 1s and one for 0s. I am going to use grey to represent 1s and black for 0s.

Place the beads onto your cord according to the binary number for each letter.

Here I have laid out the beads to represent the binary number 01000100 which represents the letter D in ASCII:

Add the rest of the beads needed to represent the rest of your initials:

Now tie your cord together and you have a bracelet!

What you're learning

Activities such as this are excellent in helping to understand how binary representation works, and in particular how it is used to represent and communicate text. Once you've tried this, why not see if you can come up with your own activity that enables you to represent ASCII in binary.

Link back to the National Curriculum for Computing:

- ◆ Design, use and evaluate computational abstractions that model the state and behaviour of real-world problems and physical systems.
- ◆ Understand how numbers can be represented in binary.

- Understand the hardware and software components that make up computer systems, and how they communicate with one another and with other systems.
- Understand how instructions are stored and executed within a computer system; understand how data of various types (including text, sounds and pictures) can be represented and manipulated digitally, in the form of binary digits.

Link back to computational thinking skills:
- Formulating instructions to achieve a desired effect.
- Formulating instructions to be followed in a given order (sequence).
- Breaking down artefacts into constituent parts to make them easier to work with.
- Identifying patterns and commonalities in artefacts.
- Adapting solutions, or parts of solutions, so they apply to a whole class of similar problems.
- Transferring ideas and solutions from one problem area to another.
- Choosing a way to represent an artefact, to allow it to be manipulated in useful ways.

Extending this activity – where next?

Binary is just one number system; computers also use one called hexadecimal. If you have access to the internet then why not have a look online to see if you can find out more about how hexadecimal works and where it is used.

Useful related online resources

Digital Schoolhouse – Three Word Stories: https://www.digitalschoolhouse.org.uk/documents/computational-word-games-three-word-stories

KITCHENS ROCK!

Find out how computers represent sound using pots and pans
> What you need:
> - A range of pots and pans – you can have as many as you like, but you should try to get at least four
> - Wooden spoons
> - Pen
> - Paper or Post-it notes

Recommended age range:
Suitable for all ages

Prior knowledge/experience:
None

What to do

Write out a sequential number for each of the pots and pans that you have chosen.

Lay out your range of pots and pans on a work surface or table and place a number in front of each pot or pan.

Each pot or pan is now labelled with a number in sequence. So if I have five pans, then they are labelled one to five.

Now write out a sequence of numbers at random, using the numbers you used to label your pans. So if you have five pans, then use the numbers one to five. For example, 1, 2, 2, 1, 5, 3, 2, 4, 3, 4, 2, 1, 1, 2.

Take your wooden spoon and hit the pots or pans in the order your sequence of numbers tells you.

Shake it up!

Try using glasses with different levels of water in each for a more tuneful experience!

Rather than using random numbers write a piece of music using the numbers for your pots and pans.

Extend this and put into practice what you've already learned by writing the numbers for each of your pots and pans in binary.

What you're learning

There is more than one way to represent sound on a computer. Whereas MP3 and Wav use binary to represent the measurement of a soundwave, MIDI uses binary to represent the note itself just like you have used a number to represent each of your pots and pans in this activity.

MIDI uses binary to represent more than just the note though; included in the MIDI message is binary to represent how hard the note was played, how long it was played for and when the note was released.

Link back to the National Curriculum for Computing:

- ◆ Design, use and evaluate computational abstractions that model the state and behaviour of real-world problems and physical systems.
- ◆ Understand how instructions are stored and executed within a computer system; understand how data of various types (including text, sounds and pictures) can be represented and manipulated digitally, in the form of binary digits.

Link back to computational thinking skills:

- ◆ Formulating instructions to achieve a desired effect.
- ◆ Formulating instructions to be followed in a given order (sequence).
- ◆ Using an appropriate notation to write code to represent any of the above.
- ◆ Identifying patterns and commonalities in artefacts.
- ◆ Reducing complexity by removing unnecessary detail.
- ◆ Choosing a way to represent an artefact, to allow it to be manipulated in useful ways.

Extending this activity – where next?

Audacity is free software that allows you to create and manipulate sound files. It's also a really useful way to be able to see and understand how computers represent sound, and how that makes it easier to manipulate.

Download the software, edit some sound files and explore the possibilities!

Useful related online resources

Audacity – Free open-source sound editing software:
https://www.audacityteam.org/

CHAPTER 5

Logical Thinking

DOT TO DOT

Join all the dots by drawing over the lines, but never go over any line more than once

What you need:

- ◆ Pens or pencils
- ◆ Worksheet
- ◆ Paper

Recommended age range:
Suitable for age eight plus

Prior knowledge/experience:
None

What to do

Copy the shapes below onto a sheet of paper and see if you can draw over every line without lifting your pencil off the paper but only using each line once.

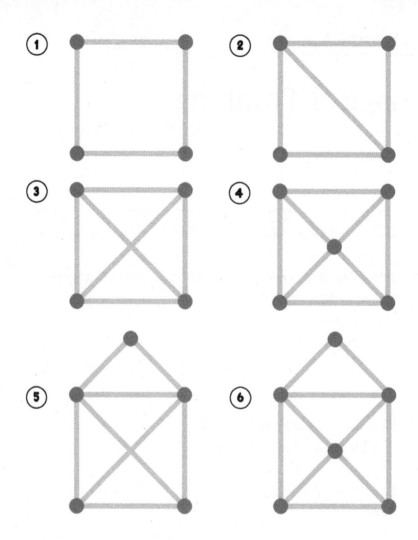

Points for discussion

Can you see a pattern? Check the number of lines connecting each dot.
What about the number of dots? Does this have an impact on whether
you can complete the task?

What you're learning

This is a task that tests your logical thinking skills. It helps to demonstrate
that sometimes the only way to solve a problem is by thinking outside the
box. The activity helps develop not just logical reasoning but also problem-

solving skills. Can you practise your algorithmic thinking skills by writing an algorithm for your solution and testing it out on others?

Extending this activity – where next?

Take a piece of A4 paper and two dice.

Roll the dice. Whatever the result of adding the two numbers is, draw that number of dots on the A4 paper. Now try and draw a line to each of the dots. You must visit each dot but only go between any two dots once. Attempt The Seven Bridges of Claydon activity below.

Useful related online resources

Super Kids – A range of ideas based around joining dots: www.superkids.com/aweb/tools/logic/dots

Solution

Images 1, 2, 5 and 6 can be drawn in one go, but they might require some practice. Images 3 and 4 can't be drawn in one go.

THE SEVEN BRIDGES OF CLAYDON

Based on the seven bridges of Königsberg. A delivery driver's nightmare!

What you need:
◆ Colouring pencils
◆ Paper
◆ Copy of the map

Recommended age range:
Suitable for age eight plus

Prior knowledge/experience:
Your child should have completed the Dot to Dot activity

What to do

The residents of Claydon have the misfortune of living on an island where two rivers join forming a larger river. Delivery drivers often have problems delivering items around the town. Their Satnav often makes them go back over several of the bridges multiple times. What they really want is a continuous route to go over each of the bridges once only.

Your task is to plan a route for the delivery drivers that delivers to all parts of the town. You cannot go over any bridge twice, but you must go over all the bridges.

You can start wherever you want:

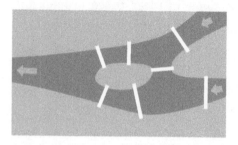

What you're learning

Problem solving is an important part of what you are doing here. You are looking at a problem and thinking how it could be solved.

The first thing you might do is abstract it. This means to remove any unwanted detail. Then you could use logical reasoning to try to explain how it could work. You might develop some simple algorithms to try and work through it and try to detect and correct errors as you progress.

Discussion points

Think about how a Satnav might work.

Consider your route from home to school. How many different routes can you take? Why do you choose the route that you do, and do you vary it sometimes? If you do vary it, then why?

What things do you think the Satnav might take into consideration when it's planning the route?

Extending this activity - where next?

Open Google Maps (or another similar tool) and enter a nearby destination. See the route that it plots. Google Maps will also often highlight alternative routes. Have a look at the different routes available. What route would you plan? What are the options that you can change? How does this affect your route?

Useful related online resources

Maths is Fun – Logic Puzzle activity:

www.mathsisfun.com/activity/seven-bridges-konigsberg.html

Solution

Try abstracting the problem. You could draw a much simpler map. Start by labelling the land and islands and numbering the bridges.

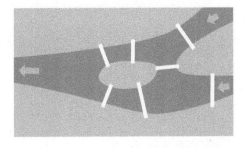

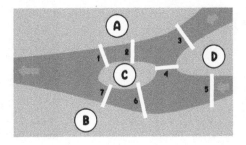

Now remove all the map detail and link together all the labels you made using letters for the landmasses and numbers for the bridges. This might help with working the problem out.

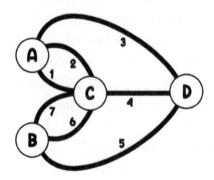

There is no solution. It is one of the great puzzles and is worth attempting because it requires you to practise your logical reasoning and abstraction skills.

I WANT TO SEE EVERYTHING!

A tourist wants to see thirteen places of interest by plane
What you need:
- ◆ Colouring pencils
- ◆ Ruler
- ◆ Paper
- ◆ Copy of the tourist's map

Recommended age range:
Eight years—adult

Prior knowledge/experience:
None

What to do

A tourist has arrived in York with a special plane ticket. The ticket only allows them to travel from one airport to another in a day and visit that place of interest for the day. They cannot follow the same route or return by it, and can only visit a place once. You are the ATTG (Aero travel tour guide) and must come up with a tour that visits thirteen of the best sites around the UK and that starts and finishes in York. The tourist has indicated on the map the places they want to visit.

Rules

You must travel in as straight a line as possible and only visit each site once. You cannot follow a route more than once or return along the same route.

What you're learning

This is another example of logical thinking. It's an important part of being a computer genius. We learn logical thinking and the more we practise this the better we become. Logical thinkers observe and analyse problems and puzzles. They then draw conclusions based on that input. They can justify their plans and decisions based on the facts they gather.

Extending this activity – where next?

Think about where you live. If you live in a city, you may have an underground, bus or tram system that gets people around. See if you can find a map of it.

See if you can create a route that visits several different places only once and only travels on a line once.

If you live in a small city or town, or in the countryside, try and do the same with the bus service.

Another challenge to think about is to find twelve different places local to you and try and plan a visit to each of them without using the same road/path twice.

Solution

There are a few ways of completing this challenge. Here's mine.

Start	York (Rufforth airfield)
Travel to	London
	Portsmouth
	Cardiff
	St Davids
	Belfast
	Edinburgh
	Liverpool
	Snowdonia
	Bath

	Oxford
	Birmingham
	Manchester
Finish	York

Useful related online resources

Teaching London Computing – The Knight's Tour Activity: https://teachinglondoncomputing.org/resources/inspiring-unplugged-classroom-activities/the-knights-tour-activity/

YOU'LL NOT GET YOUR DINNER, MR FOX!

Get to the other side of the river

    What you need:

- ◆ Colouring pencils
- ◆ Paper

or

- ◆ Any three items from around the house
- ◆ Something to represent a river

Recommended age range:
Suitable for age eight plus

Prior knowledge/experience:
None

What to do

The farmer has three things he wants to take to the market: a fox, a chicken and a sack of grain. To get to market he must cross a river in his boat, but he can only transport one item at a time. He needs to be careful what he leaves together on the banks of the river. For example, he cannot leave the chicken and the grain because the chicken will eat the grain.

Rules

The boat can only carry two items; one of those items has to be the farmer who does the rowing!

Items that cannot be left together:
Fox **AND** chicken
Chicken **AND** grain

You can either draw a fox, a chicken and a bag of grain onto three separate sheets of paper or use any three different items from around the house, for example a cup, a bag of Haribo and an apple.

Move one item at a time across the river. Which item will you move first, then move next?

What you're learning

This is logical thinking. It's an important part of being a computer genius. It's something we learn how to do and the more we practise this the better we become. Logical thinkers observe and analyse problems and puzzles. They then draw conclusions based on that input. They can justify their plans and decisions based on the facts they gather.

For example:
1. Fish live in water
2. A goldfish is a fish
3. Therefore a goldfish lives in water

Link back to the National Curriculum for Computing:
KS1
   ◆ Use logical reasoning to predict the behaviour of simple programs

KS2
   ◆ Use logical reasoning to explain how some simple algorithms work and to detect and correct errors in algorithms and programs

Discussion points
Could the rules be changed but mean the same?

What would happen if the farmer introduced an additional item, for example another chicken or another sack of grain, but the rules stayed the same?

Useful related online resources
The 7 Sisters – IT and Computing resources and activities: http://www.the7sisters.co.uk/free/pages/resource/modelling/farmer/index.html

Solution
1. Cross the river with the chicken.
2. Return with nothing, leaving the chicken behind.
3. Cross the river with the fox.
4. Return with the chicken, leaving the fox behind.
5. Cross the river with the sack of grain, leaving the chicken behind.
6. Return with nothing, leaving the sack of grain behind.
7. Cross the river with the chicken again.

WHAT'S FOR DINNER?

Develop logical skills with day-to-day events
   What you need:
   ◆ Nothing except a willingness to help next dinner time

Recommended age range:
Suitable for age eight plus

Prior knowledge/experience:
None, though it would be useful to know what ingredients go
into a dinner

What to do
Before you next sit down to a dinner with your family, encourage your
child to help to organise the ingredients before the cooking begins.

You will need to gather the ingredients and put them into the order in
which they are going to be used. A Sunday roast is great for this. Clear
some space on a counter and put all the food in order. For example, I'm
having a roast chicken so the order would be:

Chicken (roast)

Potatoes (roast)

Sweet potato, butternut squash, parsnip (roast)

Swede (boil)

Carrots (boil)

Beans (steam)

Cabbage (steam)

Gravy (make)

What you're learning
In this simple activity you are using a few computer science techniques. In programming we tend to use concepts such as sequencing

and selection and repetition. In this activity you have put all the ingredients into a sequence (order) ready for cooking. You have selected them in order based on their cooking time and thought about how some of the ingredients could be cooked at the same time.

You have used logical reasoning to put the ingredients in order much the same as a simple algorithm works. You've also detected and corrected any errors you found in this algorithm such as if two items needed putting in to the oven at the same time or two items needed cooking at the same time but used different methods such as roasting and boiling.

Extending this activity - where next?
Check out the algorithm section.

Parents, this activity could be done straight after a shopping trip where you ask your child to read the instructions on how to cook a meal and get them to sort the ingredients into an order depending on how long they need to be cooked.

Another activity could be when something is being built in the house such as a cupboard or shelf unit or a repair job.

CORNY CHICKENS!

You have three chickens and three sacks of corn to get across a river

What you need:
- Colouring pencils
- Paper

or

- Any similar items from around the house, for example three cups and three grapes
- Anything to act like a river

Recommended age range:
Suitable for age eight plus

Prior knowledge/experience:
None

What to do

The farmer has been to market and bought three chickens and three sacks of corn. He has to get them all safely across a river. He has a boat which will transport him and any two items at a time but he must be careful what he leaves together on the banks of the river. For example, he can't leave more chickens than the number of sacks of corn because the chickens will eat it all.

Rules

The boat the farmer uses has a hole in it so he must use one item to cover the hole. The boat can carry three items. One of those items has to be the farmer who does the rowing plus one item to cover the hole. He could carry two sacks of corn over but the remaining sack of corn would be eaten by the chickens.

Put your six items on one side of the table with your makeshift river down the middle.

OR

On a sheet of paper draw three chickens and on another draw three sacks of corn. Cut each one out.

Move any two of the items from one side of the river to the other. There has to be at least one item in the boat including the farmer. Then go back and move another item. Which item will you move next?

What you're learning

Logical thinking and reasoning are key parts of problem solving. The more you practise logical thinking and reasoning the better you become and the easier you'll find it.

Try this one for a bit of fun.

Isaac was looking at a photo. Someone asked him, 'Whose picture are you looking at?' He replied, 'I don't have any brother or sister, but this man's father is my father's son.' So, whose picture was Isaac looking at?

A. The man in the photo is Isaac's son. Hint: This man's father is Isaac.

Link back to the National Curriculum for Computing:
KS1

- ◆ Use logical reasoning to predict the behaviour of simple programs

KS2

- ◆ Use logical reasoning to explain how some simple algorithms work and to detect and correct errors in algorithms and programs

Extending this activity – where next?

Thinking

- ◆ What's the minimum number of moves you could make?

- What would happen if the farmer introduced an additional item, for example, another sack of corn or a chicken?
- What would the minimum number of moves be then?
- If you added an item would there be a pattern to the minimum number of moves?
- Could you write an algorithm for this puzzle?
- Could you make this puzzle for your friends to try in Scratch?

Solution

- Cross with two chickens. Leave one chicken on the bank and cross back over the river with the other chicken in the boat.
- Collect the other chicken and cross the river. Leave one of the chickens on the bank and cross back with the other.
- You should have three sacks of corn on one bank and two chickens on the other and a third in the boat.
- Leave the chicken on the bank and put two sacks of corn in the boat to cross.
- Leave both sacks of corn on the bank and bring back one of the chickens.
- Now collect the sack of corn so you are returning with one sack of corn and a chicken.
- Leave the corn on the bank and return with the chicken.
- You can now collect the remaining chicken and return to the far bank of the river with two chickens.
- No chickens were hurt and no corn eaten. Well done!

Useful online resources

Maths is Fun – Maths and Logic Puzzles: https://www.mathsisfun.com/puzzles/

IT'S TEA TIME, GO AND WASH YOUR HANDS

Thinking about how computers work by washing your hands

What you need:

◆ Soap and water

Recommended age range:
Suitable for ages eight to eleven

Prior knowledge/experience:
None except how to wash your hands!

What to do

Go and wash your hands with soap, dry them and come back!

What you're learning

Here, you are learning about logic gates, which are the bricks and mortar of digital products. They work by taking one or more binary inputs to produce a single output. These operations make all digital devices do their thing.

AND gates

The inputs are A & B. the output is R.

In the 'Wash your hands' activity the inputs were soap and water and the output would be clean hands (and tea!)

The best way to think of an AND gate is *'if this **AND** this are on then it will work'.* Now think about how you washed your hands. If you turned the tap on **AND** got your hands wet **AND** used soap, you would have washed your hands. If you just used soap but no water then you would have soapy hands which would still be grubby, or if you just used water then your hands would just be wet and not clean. If you used neither, your hands would still be grubby.

Link back to the National Curriculum for Computing:
KS3

♦ Understand simple Boolean logic [for example, AND, OR and NOT] and some of its uses in circuits and programming.

Extending this activity – where next?

Mum wants a cup of tea. To make a cup of tea you must have a tea bag and boiling water. Just having a tea bag in the cup is not a cup of tea and just having boiling water in the cup is not a cup of tea. Now, go make mum a cup of tea!

A slightly more conventional use of the **AND** gate is looking at a boiler system. There are two sensors near the top. One monitors whether there is enough water in the tank while the other senses if the water is cold. They both send signals to a heater that will only work if it gets a signal from both sensors. There must be enough water AND the water must be cold. If it only gets one signal, it won't do anything. The signal from the sensors can be shown in binary as 1 being on and 0 as being off, meaning there is no signal.

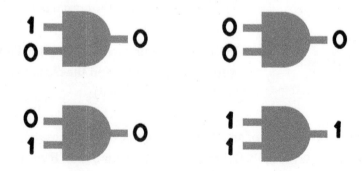

What other examples can you find around your house? Sky box AND television? Both need to be on in order for you to watch the telly? Both the PlayStation AND controller are required for you to move a character. You need bread AND filling to make a sandwich.

Useful related online resources

Logic.ly – Create virtual logic gates and simulate circuits:
  https://logic.ly/flash/
Think Maths – Using dominoes to create logic gates and other computer operations:
  http://www.think-maths.co.uk/downloads/domino-computer-worksheets

Extending this activity – OR gates

1) Can you arrange a set of LEGO pieces to create the AND gate shape?
2) Look at the shapes and the way AND gates work in the explanation above. Using a set of dominoes, can you arrange them so that that they mimic the way the AND gate works. For example, both input chains will need to fall in order for the output chain to drop. *Note, the AND gate is perhaps the trickiest to recreate using dominoes.*

<u>OR gates</u>

The inputs are A and B. the output is R.

In the 'Wash your hands' activity, the inputs were water AND soap, and the output was clean hands. However, it didn't matter if the water was hot OR cold. You would get clean hands regardless of the temperature of the water used.

The best way to think of an OR gate is to think 'if this OR this is on then it will work'.

Think about this; you want to wash your hands. If either the hot tap OR cold tap are on OR both of them are on, you can get your hands wet and wash them. If none of the taps are on then no water comes out and you can't wash your hands!

The screen on your phone might work if you press the on button OR put your finger on the biometric scanner OR both. But it won't work if none of them are pressed.

A slightly more conventional use of the OR gate is looking at a burglar alarm system. There are two sensors (inputs), one on the window and another on the door, and an alarm (output). If neither of the sensors are activated the alarm is quiet. If the window is opened OR the door is opened OR both are opened then the alarm will sound.

The signal from the sensors can be shown in binary as 1 being on and 0 as being off, meaning there is no signal.

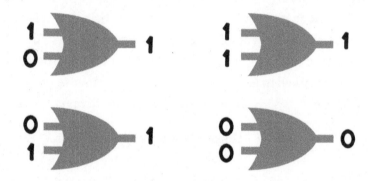

What to do

1) What other examples can you find around your house of OR gate systems? How about a sandwich? Bread with cheese OR pickle OR both makes a sandwich. But if you don't put anything in, it's just a couple of slices of bread.

2) Look at the shape of the OR gate above. Can you recreate an OR gate with LEGO pieces?

3) Can you arrange domino pieces so that they work like an OR gate? You should have two input lines and a single output line (the dominoes at the end of the chain), which should drop regardless of which initial domino piece is dropped first.

Useful related online resources

Logic.ly – Create virtual logic gates and simulate circuits:
   https://logic.ly/flash/

Think Maths – Using dominoes to create logic gates and other computer operations:
   http://www.think-maths.co.uk/downloads/domino-computer-worksheets

---

DOES THE LIGHT REALLY GO OFF IN THE FRIDGE?

Thinking about how computers work by opening the fridge door
   What you need:
   ◆ A fridge

Recommended age range:
Suitable for ages eight to eleven

Prior knowledge/experience:
None but it's useful to remember what the logic gates are

What to do

Go and open the fridge door, or any door in your house where a light comes on when the door is open!

Discussion points
   ◆ Is the light always on?
   ◆ When does the light come on?
   ◆ How does the fridge 'know' when to switch the light on and off?
   ◆ Sensors help computers to 'sense' the outside world. For example a thermometer measures temperature, and a temperature sensor can help to keep greenhouses and

your home warm. What type of sensor do you think your fridge might use and where do you think it might be? How do you think it helps to control the light?

What you're learning

Logic gates control all sorts of systems around us and computers use logic for almost everything they do. Therefore, understanding the main constructs is really important. You've already learned about the AND and OR gates. Now it's time to learn about the NOT gate.

NOT gates

The input is A. The output is R.

When opening the fridge, the input is a sensor on the door and the output is to switch on the light.

The NOT gate is different from AND and OR gates. It only has one input and the output is always opposite to it. It is therefore also called an inverter.

The best way to think of a NOT gate is: 'whatever signal goes in, the opposite will come out'.

Think about the fridge door. If the door is open, the light is on. If the door is closed, the light is off. (Honestly it is, I put a camera in mine to check!)

Link back to the National Curriculum for Computing:
KS3

◆ Understand simple Boolean logic [for example, AND, OR and NOT] and some of its uses in circuits and programming.

Extending this activity – where next?

There are many examples of NOT gates around the house and outside. A good one is a car door. If the car door is open, the interior light stays on. If it is closed, the light goes out.

The signal from the sensors can be shown in binary as 1 meaning there is a signal and 0 meaning there is no signal. The NOT gate simply reverses or gives you the opposite of whatever the input signal is. So an input of 0 (i.e. the door is open) gives out an output of 1 (so the light is on).

What other examples can you find around your house? How about: if you don't put Marmite on toast, you get nice toast. If you do put Marmite on toast, you get nasty toast! Or perhaps it's the other way around for you?

Remember: there must be an exact opposite of the input for the NOT gate. For example, if you were playing Guess Who, saying 'NOT Male' would then only show the females. Or it's the equivalent of saying if the switch is 'off' then the light is 'on'.

What to do

1) What other examples can you find around your house of NOT gate systems?
2) Look at the shape of the NOT gate above. Can you recreate a NOT gate with LEGO pieces?

Useful related online resources

Logic.ly – Create virtual logic gates and simulate circuits:
   https://logic.ly/flash/
BBC Bitesize – talking about logic gates:
   https://www.bbc.co.uk/bitesize/clips/zwmf34j

....

CHAPTER 6

Memory and Storage

PAPER DISCS

Learn about storage capacity with this fun activity using only paper discs

What you need:

- ◆ Paper
- ◆ Scissors
- ◆ Pens or pencils

Recommended age range:
Suitable for all ages

Prior knowledge/experience:
None

What to do

Use the paper you have gathered and cut out three squares with the following measurements:

0.7cm x 0.7cm
4.5cm x 4.5cm
25cm x 25cm

Label the back of the smallest square 'CD', the middle size 'DVD', and the largest piece 'Blu-Ray'.

Taking each piece of paper in turn, trace as much as possible of the following image into the space available and colour it in with materials you have around you. Don't scale the image or try to make it fit. See what you can draw without changing the image.

Once you have drawn these, create three more squares of the required sizes and label them the same. This time try drawing the house in full within each square.

What you're learning

Each piece of paper represents the difference in storage capacity between CDs, DVDs and Blu-Ray discs. The drawings represent the difference in the amount of information that can be stored within each disc, and also the compression that would be needed to store the full information in each.

Discuss how much you had to shrink the image of the house to make it fit the square. When you shrank it, was it as good as the original? Did you lose any detail? There are different ways to compress computer data, and sometimes it can result in reduced quality. For example, images sent over WhatsApp are always compressed. You can test this for yourself. If you have an image on your phone, send it over email and then through WhatsApp as well. Download both files onto a computer and compare their file sizes. You'll notice that the image received via WhatsApp will be significantly smaller.

Link back to the National Curriculum for Computing:
KS1

- Use technology purposefully to create, organise, store, manipulate and retrieve digital content.
- Recognise common uses of information technology beyond school.
- Use technology safely and respectfully, keeping personal information private; identify where to go for help and support when they have concerns about content or contact on the internet or other online technologies.

KS2

- Select, use and combine a variety of software (including internet services) on a range of digital devices.
- Use technology safely, respectfully and responsibly.

KS3

- Understand the hardware and software components that make up computer systems, and how they communicate with one another and with other systems.
- Understand how instructions are stored and executed within a computer system.
- Understand a range of ways to use technology safely, respectfully, responsibly and securely.

Link back to computational thinking skills:

Abstraction

- ◆ Reducing complexity by removing unnecessary detail.
- ◆ Choosing a way to represent an artefact, to allow it to be manipulated in useful ways.
- ◆ Filtering information when developing solutions.

Useful related online resources

Teaching London Computing – Compression Code Puzzles:
https://teachinglondoncomputing.org/compression-code-puzzles/

CS Unplugged – Text compression:
https://classic.csunplugged.org/text-compression/

SPACE-SAVER

Learn about the uses of primary and secondary storage whilst organising your home and getting ready for school

What you need:

- ◆ Pencil
- ◆ Paper
- ◆ Fridge and freezer
- ◆ Toys/games
- ◆ School bag and books

Recommended age range:
Age five upwards

Prior knowledge/experience:
Should have completed the Paper Discs activity

What to do

In our daily lives there are many scenarios that require us to think about what things are most relevant to our current routine. It isn't practical to carry everything we own around with us just in case. So, what do we do? We store some things away somewhere for later when we will need them. A few scenarios around the house might include:

1. Helping to store food appropriately

Some food is needed today or tomorrow, so it is kept in the fridge (short-term storage), whereas some may be needed next week so it is kept in the freezer (long-term storage) to make sure it stays fresh!

Next time your parents bring home the shopping, help them out and think carefully about what should go in the fridge and what should go in the freezer.

2. Tidying around the house

Over the years the number of toys, games and books you own may well increase and eventually you may run out of space to keep them all. You don't need all of them out at once, so think carefully about those you most enjoy using at the moment. These could be kept in your bedroom, readily available, and the rest stored safely away in an attic or garage.

3. Getting ready for school

An important part of the day is making sure that you have everything you need for school. You can't carry every exercise book, textbook or other equipment you own all the time, so you keep some at home until you need them. Next time you're getting ready for school, think carefully about what is needed on that day, and what can be left behind at home.

What you're learning

Primary storage refers to storage that contains data that is actively being used at that time, whereas secondary storage refers to data that is not currently in use. Therefore, primary storage is temporary (volatile) while secondary storage is permanent.

Each of the three scenarios above (i.e. Helping to store food appropriately, Tidying the house and Getting ready for school) are a representation of **primary storage**, such as **Random Access Memory (RAM)** or **Read-only Memory (ROM)**, as well as **secondary storage** such as your **Hard Disk Drive (HDD)** or **Solid State Drive (SSD)**. As we've said, primary storage is used to store information about programs or systems currently in use and secondary storage is used to store information we don't need right now. So when you are using your computer, the work you are currently doing is saved in RAM. If you want to open up the story you wrote last week, then you will be accessing that from the HDD or SSD (secondary storage). The examples are explained below:

Primary storage	Secondary storage
Random Access Memory	Hard Disk Drive
Fridge	Freezer
Bedroom	Attic/Garage
School bag	Home

Link back to the National Curriculum for Computing:

KS1

- ◆ Use technology purposefully to organise, store and retrieve digital content.
- ◆ Recognise common uses of information technology beyond school.

KS2

- Select, use and combine a variety of software (including Internet services) on a range of digital devices.

KS3

- Understand the hardware and software components that make up computer systems.

Link back to computational thinking skills:

Abstraction

- Reducing complexity by removing unnecessary detail.
- Choosing a way to represent an artefact to allow it to be manipulated in useful ways.
- Filtering information when developing solutions.

Decomposition

- Breaking down a problem into simpler versions of the same problem that can be solved in the same way.

Extending this activity – where next?

Next time you're using a computer or a smartphone, take a look at what programs are currently running. Think about the amount of storage you're using up when you have five apps open, or ten, or even fifteen. Does anything happen to the speed of your phone or computer when you have too many open? Our primary storage is often a lot smaller than our secondary so make sure you're stopping programs or apps fully when they're not in use and you'll find things run a lot more smoothly.

Can you think of any more example scenarios, at home or anywhere else, where this concept is used? Copy or complete the table below with all the examples you can think of!

Primary storage	Secondary storage
Random Access Memory	*Hard Disk Drive*

STORAGE TRUMP CARDS

Learn about the benefits of a variety of storage solutions whilst making a fun game for you and your family!

What you need:

♦ Colouring pencils

♦ Paper or card

♦ Scissors

Recommended age range:
Age seven upwards

Prior knowledge/experience:
You need to have completed the Space-saver activity

What to do

Think about all the digital systems used within your house that store some form of information: USB sticks, computer hard drives, cloud software (such as OneDrive or Google Drive), mobile phones, CDs, DVDs, etc. Find as many as you can think of that are currently inside your house and give them a ranking out of five in the following categories:

- ◆ Storage capacity
- ◆ Speed
- ◆ Portability
- ◆ Durability
- ◆ Reliability
- ◆ Cost

Your task is to create Top Trumps cards based on these devices. Be creative in your search, think carefully about any digital system storing information.

Device		Device		Device	
Storage capacity	OOOOO	Storage capacity	OOOOO	Storage capacity	OOOOO
Speed	OOOOO	Speed	OOOOO	Speed	OOOOO
Portability	OOOOO	Portability	OOOOO	Portability	OOOOO
Durability	OOOOO	Durability	OOOOO	Durability	OOOOO
Reliability	OOOOO	Reliability	OOOOO	Reliability	OOOOO
Cost	OOOOO	Cost	OOOOO	Cost	OOOOO

Device		Device		Device	
Storage capacity	OOOOO	Storage capacity	OOOOO	Storage capacity	OOOOO
Speed	OOOOO	Speed	OOOOO	Speed	OOOOO
Portability	OOOOO	Portability	OOOOO	Portability	OOOOO
Durability	OOOOO	Durability	OOOOO	Durability	OOOOO
Reliability	OOOOO	Reliability	OOOOO	Reliability	OOOOO
Cost	OOOOO	Cost	OOOOO	Cost	OOOOO

What you're learning

Learning more about various storage devices, how they work, how reliable they are, how much they can store and more will help you make better decisions when considering your own purchases in future. It will help you know what size phone to buy if you prefer to use it for photos instead of music, or what type of hard drive to get if you're a keen gamer.

Link back to the National Curriculum for Computing:
KS1

◆ Use technology purposefully to create, organise, store, manipulate and retrieve digital content.

KS3

◆ Understand the hardware and software components that make up computer systems, and how they communicate with one another and with other systems.
◆ Design, use and evaluate computational abstractions that model the state and behaviour of real-world problems and physical systems.

Link back to computational thinking skills:
Decomposition

◆ Breaking down artefacts into constituent parts to make them easier to work with.
◆ Breaking down a problem into simpler versions of the same problem that can be solved in the same way (recursive and divide-and-conquer strategies).

Generalisation (Patterns)

◆ Identifying patterns and commonalities in artefacts.

Abstraction

- Reducing complexity by removing unnecessary detail.
- Hiding the full complexity of an artefact (hiding functional complexity).
- Hiding complexity in data, for example by using data structures.
- Filtering information when developing solutions.

Evaluation

- Assessing that an artefact is fit for purpose.
- Assessing whether the performance of an artefact is good enough (utility: effectiveness and efficiency).
- Comparing the performance of artefacts that do the same thing.
- Assessing whether a product meets general performance criteria (heuristics).

Extending this activity - where next?

As an additional step, try researching even more specific information for the devices and make an advanced mode for your game. Investigate whether the storage is optical, magnetic or solid state. Try and find out the read-and-write speed, actual cost and so on. Explain some of the limitations of these devices as well as the benefits.

Useful related online resources

BBC Bitesize – GCSE Computer Science – Data Storage (Sections 5-6):
https://www.bbc.com/bitesize/guides/z7rk7ty/revision/5

VIRTUAL LEGO

Use LEGO to discover how computers run multiple programs at once

What you need:

- ◆ 2 x LEGO baseplate
- ◆ Assorted LEGO bricks
- ◆ Dice

Recommended age range:
Suitable for all ages

Prior knowledge/experience:
Your child should have completed the Space-saver activity

What to do

Set two LEGO baseplates on your table. Label one as RAM and the other as Virtual. If one of your baseplates is smaller than the other, label the smaller one RAM.

Collect your LEGO bricks, organise them by colour and select a type of program for each colour to represent out of the following:

- ◆ Office programs (Word, PowerPoint, Excel)
- ◆ Web browsers (Internet Explorer, Chrome, Firefox)
- ◆ Media streaming (video/audio)
- ◆ Photo editing (Photoshop/Paint)
- ◆ Gaming

Make sure your different bricks have the correct amount of LEGO studs available:

Program Category	# of LEGO Studs	Dice Roll
Office programs	4	1
Web browsers	6	2

Media streaming	8	3
Photo streaming	10	4
Gaming	12	5

Roll a dice and place a full program based on the number rolled. For example, if you roll a 3 you will need to place 8 studs' worth of LEGO in a single colour on the base plate. The more you roll, the more the plate should fill up.

All the LEGO bricks should be added in a single layer. Do not build on top of bricks already laid on the baseplate. If you roll and there is not enough room to place the bricks on the RAM baseplate, move the fewest number of LEGO bricks from the RAM baseplate over to the Virtual baseplate to make room for the new program.

What you're learning

When you run multiple programs on a digital device, the device stores currently used information in its Random Access Memory (RAM); however, if you open too many programs then the device will use its secondary storage (HDD/SDD) to store the information as virtual memory. Here we're representing programs as multi-coloured bricks and showing the need for the computer to store certain information and how this can slow the computer down by moving data from RAM into virtual memory when loading programs.

Link back to the National Curriculum for Computing:

KS1

- Use technology purposefully to create, organise, store, manipulate and retrieve digital content.
- Recognise common uses of information technology beyond school.
- Use technology safely and respectfully, keeping personal information private; identify where to go for help and support when they have concerns about content or contact on the internet or other online technologies.

KS2

- Select, use and combine a variety of software (including internet services) on a range of digital devices.
- Use technology safely, respectfully and responsibly.

KS3

- Understand the hardware and software components that make up computer systems, and how they communicate with one another and with other systems.
- Understand how instructions are stored and executed within a computer system.
- Understand a range of ways to use technology safely, respectfully, responsibly and securely.

Link back to computational thinking skills:

Abstraction

- Reducing complexity by removing unnecessary detail.
- Choosing a way to represent an artefact, to allow it to be manipulated in useful ways.
- Filtering information when developing solutions.

Useful related online resources

BBC Bitesize – Search "CPU and Memory" > Section 8

VOLATILE (RE)VISION

Revise for your favourite school topics whilst learning about the difference between volatile and non-volatile memory

What you need:

- Pens or pencils
- Paper
- Scissors

Recommended age range:
Suitable for all ages

Prior knowledge/experience:
None

What to do

Select a topic you're learning about at school and want to test your memory on. This could be any subject and any topic you like.

Cut out ten small pieces of paper, big enough to write key terms, phrases, spellings or definitions on.

Mark five of these with one colour or symbol and write information that you are particularly struggling with and may need additional reminders to remember properly.

The other five pieces of paper should be marked with a different colour or symbol and contain information that you feel more confident with and only need a little testing on.

Review your revision cards with somebody else and get them to test your knowledge. Do so for between five and ten minutes to see how well you do.

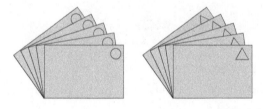

Once you've finished, take the five cards that you are more confident with and put them to one side, safe for the next day. The cards you're less confident with, however, should be ripped up and thrown away. Tomorrow, come back to the cards and try rewriting those that you discarded in order to test your knowledge. Can you manage to complete them all without any help? Can you discard different ones each day to test your knowledge properly? Perhaps somebody else could select the discarded cards?

What you're learning

Computers store information in a variety of ways and two examples of those are Read-only Memory (ROM) and Random Access Memory (RAM).

ROM is an example of non-volatile memory, meaning the computer does not lose information stored here even when it is turned off. We represent this with the cards we select to keep in between sessions.

RAM, on the other hand, is an example of volatile memory. Volatile memory does lose data when the power is turned off and is represented here by the cards we discard in between sessions.

We store crucial information in our ROM, which typically cannot be changed, so make sure your cards are correct!

Link back to the National Curriculum for Computing:
KS1

- Use technology purposefully to create, organise, store, manipulate and retrieve digital content.
- Recognise common uses of information technology beyond school.
- Use technology safely and respectfully, keeping personal information private; identify where to go for help and support when they have concerns about content or contact on the internet or other online technologies.

KS2

- Select, use and combine a variety of software (including internet services) on a range of digital devices.
- Use technology safely, respectfully and responsibly.

KS3

- Understand the hardware and software components that make up computer systems, and how they communicate with one another and with other systems.
- Understand how instructions are stored and executed within a computer system.
- Understand a range of ways to use technology safely, respectfully, responsibly and securely.

Link back to computational thinking skills:

Abstraction

- Reducing complexity by removing unnecessary detail.
- Choosing a way to represent an artefact to allow it to be manipulated in useful ways.
- Filtering information when developing solutions.

Extending this activity – where next?

As you progress and are becoming more and more confident with your chosen subjects or topics, try creating even more cards and storing less in between sessions. This added challenge will be an effective way to revise anything for an upcoming test or exam.

Useful related online resources

Digital Schoolhouse – Three Word Stories (hardware):
https://www.digitalschoolhouse.org.uk/documents/computational
-word-games-three-word-stories

CHAPTER 7

Programming

DOTTY BOXES

Use the classic game of Dots and Boxes to develop computational thinking skills

What you need:
- ◆ Rules – listed below
- ◆ Two players
- ◆ 5 x 5 grid
- ◆ Writing device

Recommended age range:
Suitable for all ages

Prior knowledge/experience:
Your child must understand what algorithms are and how they work

What to do

Dots and Boxes is a classic game underpinned by mathematical principles. Strategic thinking is key in this game as it's easy to lose a string of boxes to your opponent and thereby potentially lose the game. Likewise, small losses can result in greater wins. This game of strategic problem solving is a great way to practise those computational thinking skills. In this activity we take the game further by drawing clear links to algorithmic thinking and other computational thinking techniques.

Play a short game of Dots and Boxes. You can use the grid provided below or draw your own. The rules are:

1. The players take it in turns to draw a vertical or horizontal line between two dots.
2. The player who completes the fourth side of the box earns a point and takes another turn.
3. The game ends when no more lines can be placed.

The winner is the player with the most boxes (points).

How is the game played? Can you write a more detailed set of instructions for the game that a robot could follow? For example . . .

Sample instructions for completing the activity:
- Decide who plays first
- Player one: Connect any two dots with a vertical or horizontal line
- Has a box been closed?
  ○ If yes, then player writes initial inside square and takes an extra turn
  ○ If no, it is the next player's turn
- Player two: Connect any two dots with a vertical or horizontal line
- Has a box been closed?
  ○ If yes, then player writes initial inside square and takes an extra turn
  ○ If not, it is the next player's turn

1. Can you write the instructions in a more effective way? Can you see repeating instructions? How would you write the algorithm to prevent any from repeating unnecessarily?
2. Can you arrange the instructions in a more effective way? How about using a diagram or a flowchart? Does that make the instructions easier to understand and follow?
3. Who can write the instructions in the most accurate and effective way possible? Have a competition amongst yourselves. How will you test to see who has won? Think about your 'success criteria'. What will make one algorithm better than the other? Perhaps the accuracy?
4. Do the instructions contain enough detail? If a robot were to follow the instructions, would they know how to 'decide who plays first'? Do a separate group of instructions need to be written for this that explains it in more detail? For example, you may toss a coin, or start with the oldest person in the group.

Time to become a game designer

Change the game! Take any three instructions or game rules and change them. Now write the new instructions for the game.

Does it work? Give your instructions to someone else. Can they play the game? Could they follow the instructions properly? You may need to modify your instructions.

Once you've played the new version, you'll discover you've developed a totally new game. Congratulations, you're a game designer!

What you're learning

This activity can be carried out at any stage and is certainly worth repeating after the other activities in this chapter have been carried out. Writing the algorithm is a great way of practising different programming constructs. Being able to use iteration (repetition), for example, will help you write a better algorithm. The sample instructions given above use selection statements, which are very common for branching programming code.

Children are encouraged to consider the effectiveness of their instructions, testing them on other people and refining accordingly. This emulates the testing, debugging and evaluation stages of systems design. Changing the three instructions begins to introduce game design concepts as well and can be a great starting point for further development.

This activity supports all Key Stages within the national curriculum, as each stage outlines the coverage of core programming concepts.

Discussion points

◆ How could this game be improved?

◆ What other options could we include in this game?

Extending this activity – where next?

Consider the process you just went through:

1. Play a game
2. Write the algorithm (the instructions for how to play the game)
3. Test and refine the algorithm
4. Modify your algorithm to change any three rules
5. Test and refine your new game

This follows a typical cycle for developing new software (design > create > evaluate). We can apply this process to most areas of development. How about trying it with a new game. Follow this model with a game of snap or maybe even a game of noughts and crosses.

Give your new game a name and share it with some friends.

Useful related online resources

Digital Schoolhouse – Code Kingdoms Board Game:
   https://www.digitalschoolhouse.org.uk/documents/code-kingdoms
   -board-game

Resource

5 x 5 grids for initial game

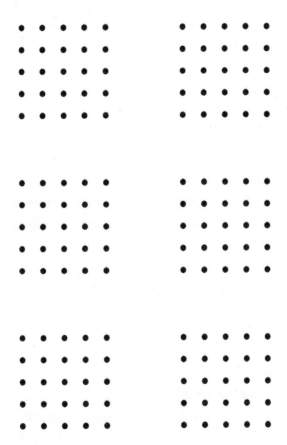

CREATING A PIZZA: SELECTION

Understand basic selection statements in programming by making a pizza for tea!

What you need:
- Tortilla or wraps
- Pizza toppings, such as mushrooms, chopped meat, pineapple, mozzarella, chopped tomatoes and any other toppings of your choice
- 1 tablespoon olive oil
- 1 tablespoon passata
- 1 garlic clove
- Baking tray
- Tablespoon
- Oven gloves

Recommended age range:
Suitable for all ages – children under the age of twelve will need an adult to help with the oven and chopping the toppings

Prior knowledge/experience:
Your child must understand what algorithms are and how they work

What to do

Preparing to make the pizza:
- Ensure you have tortilla or wraps for the pizza base
- Make sure you have the correct ingredients for the pizza
- Ensure you have toppings, chopped by a parent if needed
- Preheat your oven to the temperature listed below. Parents must supervise this instruction

Instructions for making one tortilla pizza:

- Preheat the oven to 240°C (220°C for fan-assisted ovens or gas mark 8)
- Spray 3 tbsp olive oil onto a baking tray
- Spray/rub 1 tbsp olive oil onto the tortilla base
- If you like garlic, rub this onto the tortilla base (optional)
- Add a thin layer of passata sauce onto each tortilla base
- If you like mushrooms, add them to the pizza base (optional)
- If you like ham, add it to the pizza base (optional)
- If you like pineapple, add it to the pizza base (optional)
- If you like cheese, add it to the pizza base (optional)
- Add any of your favourite toppings to the pizza base
- Put the pizza into the oven for around six minutes or until the tortilla has golden-brown edges
- Leave to cool for one minute
- Add some basil (optional)
- Eat and enjoy

Discussion points

1) Where has the word 'IF' been used?
2) Why does including the word 'IF' make the recipe (algorithm) more effective? What does it allow the chef to do?
   - **Possible answer:** It allows the chef to follow a slightly different set of instructions if a certain condition/criterion is true. In programming this is called 'branching'.
3) Think about going to the shop to spend your pocket money to buy a chocolate bar. You have £1. You notice that your favourite drink is on offer and both are £1 each. What would you do?
   - **Possible answer: Make a decision** on whether you will be buying the chocolate bar or the drink.
4) What decisions do you need to think about when making the pizza?
   - **Possible answer:** If you want a wrap or tortilla base; If you

want garlic on the base of the pizza; What types of toppings you would like on the pizza

What you're learning

In programming, the term selection is used to mean making a decision.

We make decisions on a daily basis. For example:
If it is Friday, **then** get up at 7am for school. **If** it is Saturday, **then** get up at 8am.
If it is raining, **then** I need to wear my coat, **else** I can wear a jumper.
If there is milk in the fridge, **then** I can have cereal for breakfast, **else** I will get some toast.
Programs will need to make decisions based on certain criteria. **Selection** in programming uses **IF** statements. **ELSE** is used if the original criterion is not met – for example:
If it is your birthday, say 'Happy Birthday'.
Else 'It is not my birthday yet'.

Attempt to draw a flowchart for your pizza recipe. How will you represent the decisions that need to be made?

Link back to the National Curriculum for Computing:
KS2

- ◆ Design, write and debug programs that accomplish specific goals, including controlling or simulating physical systems; solve problems by decomposing them into smaller parts.
- ◆ Use sequence, selection, and repetition in programs; work with variables and various forms of input and output.
- ◆ Use logical reasoning to explain how some simple algorithms work and to detect and correct errors in algorithms and programs.

KS3

- Design, use and evaluate computational abstractions that model the state and behaviour of real-world problems and physical systems.
- Understand several key algorithms that reflect computational thinking [for example, ones for sorting and searching]; use logical reasoning to compare the utility of alternative algorithms for the same problem.

Link back to computational thinking skills:

- Decomposition – you are breaking the overall pizza down into its smaller component parts. For example, thinking about the base separately allows you to make certain decisions about how you want the base; with the same being done for the toppings.
- Algorithmic thinking – you are following an algorithm for a pizza recipe and you could write your own.
- Generalisation – now that you know how to make a pizza you can easily keep to the same pattern but change small details to make a completely different pizza.

Extending this activity – where next?

Choose another favourite family recipe. Can you convert it into a flowchart that uses selection statements? For example, you could create a salad flowchart with different branching pathways depending on IF the salad is a Greek Salad or a Caesar Salad, and so on.

Having one large flowchart for all different possible salad types and their variations might get quite complex. How can you write yours to ensure it continues to be easy to read?

Hint: Sometimes developers break large flowcharts down into multiple smaller ones that connect together.

Useful related online resources

Digital Schoolhouse – Guess Who (a game about selection):

https://www.digitalschoolhouse.org.uk/documents/guess-who

Pizza Algorithm Design – possible solution:

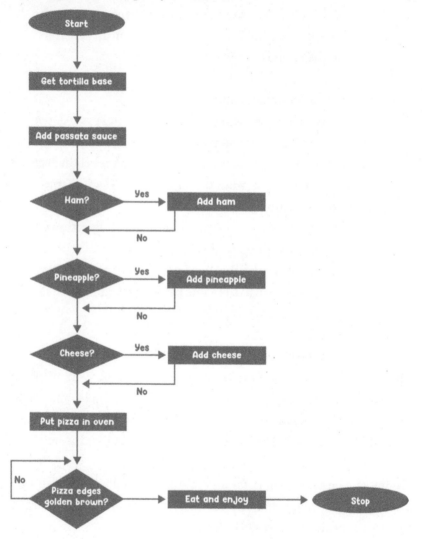

What to do

Procedures are algorithms that perform a specific task. When creating a procedure, we write the algorithm and assign it a name. Then, the next time we wish to perform that task, we can simply use the procedure name rather than writing out the entire algorithm again. They save lots of time in programming.

We use the same concept in our everyday lives. For example, when your parent tells you to 'go and make your bed', that's all they say. They expect you to understand the specific instructions involved in 'making your bed'. They don't repeat them every single time.

For example, try this:

Make your bed:
- ◆ Parent discussion:
  - ○ What is involved with making a bed?
  - ○ How many instructions do you need to perform to make a bed?
  - ○ Ask your parent/s to evaluate your bed-making ability and to give you a grade

Instructions on making a bed:
- ◆ Ensure the sheet is on all four corners of the mattress
- ◆ Tuck under any excess sheet on the sides of the mattress
- ◆ Ensure the pillow is inside its case
- ◆ Add the pillow to the top end of the bed (the end where you normally sleep)
- ◆ Ensure the duvet has its cover on and place this over the sheet
- ◆ Tuck in the duvet to the sides of the bed
- ◆ Place teddy on top of bed (optional)

Explore this concept further by completing the worksheet below with other everyday examples.

Discussion points
- ◆ Think about the sequence of instructions to make a bed
- ◆ What other procedures can you think of that you might use on a daily basis? Examples include putting on shoes, hoovering, dusting
- ◆ Parents to provide feedback on bed-making skills to child

Extending this activity – where next?

Look back at the previous activity. If you carried out the extension activity, you will have a flowchart for different salad types. Have a look at this flowchart and see if you can work out which parts of the flowchart could reflect different procedures.

Hint: Each salad could be a separate procedure. You could then create a new algorithm that decides which day of the week you would make each salad. For example IF it is Monday THEN make a Caesar Salad.

Can you use a free programming environment to turn this into a computer program?

Useful related online resources

Scratch, a free block-based programming environment:
   https://scratch.mit.edu/
Python, a free text-based programming environment:
   https://www.python.org/
Tynker, coding for kids: https://www.tynker.com/

Worksheet

Think about writing everyday procedures. We give them a name, but they include many additional instructions like making a bed. There are also other everyday procedures like making a sandwich or doing up shoelaces. Have a go with the activities below:

Procedure name:

Getting a glass of water

List all the necessary instructions for getting a glass of water:

Get a glass from the cupboard
Turn on the tap
Pour water into glass
Turn off the tap

Procedure name:

Brushing teeth

List all the necessary instructions for brushing your teeth:

Procedure name:

Tidy away toys

Add in your own instructions:

Create your own procedures

Procedure name:

Add in your own instructions:

```
_____
_____
_____
_____
_____
_____
_____
```

Procedure name:

Add in your own instructions:

```
_____
_____
_____
_____
_____
_____
_____
```

Solutions

Think about writing everyday procedures. We give them a name, but they include many additional instructions. There are also other everyday procedures like making a sandwich or doing up shoelaces. Have a go with the activity below:

Procedures:

Procedure name:
Brushing teeth

List all the necessary instructions for brushing your teeth:

Get toothbrush
Get toothpaste
Put toothpaste onto brush
Brush all your teeth
Spit out toothpaste
Put toothpaste away
Put toothbrush away

DANCING CHARACTER: PROGRAMMING

Understand how a basic program works by creating a dance for a character

What you need:
- Character template with the necessary split pins (depending on how many joints you decide to include, you will need between five and ten, one for each joint to enable the character to move its arms, legs and head)
- Flowchart
- Access to a favourite song

Recommended age range:
Suitable for all ages

Prior knowledge/experience:
Your child must understand what algorithms are and how they work, as well as key concepts including sequences, selection, iteration and procedures

What to do

Preparing to make the character:

- Copy the image of the character below onto card and cut it out
- Put the character together with the split pins. The pins go in the holes, make sure they match up
- Test the character to see that the arms and legs can move freely

Instructions on making a dancing character:

- Ensure the character is constructed and the arms and legs are able to move freely
- Pick a song that you like and listen to it a couple of times
- Whilst listening to the song think about some potential dance moves that would suit the song
- Using the activity sheets from the Dancing Algorithms activity (p.34), start adding each dance move
- Include selection; for example, would the character start dancing if there was no music?
- Include a loop. How many times does a specific dance move need repeating, for example clapping three times.
- Complete at least one procedure

What you're learning

This is a simple way to practise the programming concepts that you've been learning so far. Try to use a range of different concepts to make your dance routine more complex. No doubt you'll need to test the program to see if it works, and you'll need to go through your algorithm to try and spot and correct errors; this is known as debugging.

Link back to the National Curriculum for Computing:

KS1

- Understand what algorithms are, how they are implemented as programs on digital devices, and that programs execute by following precise and unambiguous instructions.
- Create and debug simple programs.
- Use logical reasoning to predict the behaviour of simple programs.

KS2

- Design, write and debug programs that accomplish specific goals, including controlling or simulating physical systems; solve problems by decomposing them into smaller parts.
- Use sequence, selection and repetition in programs; work with variables and various forms of input and output.
- Use logical reasoning to explain how some simple algorithms work and to detect and correct errors in algorithms and programs.

KS3

- Design, use and evaluate computational abstractions that model the state and behaviour of real-world problems and physical systems.
- Understand several key algorithms that reflect computational thinking [for example, ones for sorting and searching]; use logical reasoning to compare the utility of alternative algorithms for the same problem.
- Use two or more programming languages, at least one of which is textual, to solve a variety of computational

problems; make appropriate use of data structures [for example, lists, tables or arrays]; design and develop modular programs that use procedures or functions.

Link back to computational thinking skills:
- Algorithmic thinking
- Decomposition
- Abstraction
- Generalisation

Discussion points
- Can dancing really be a program?
- What would happen if you performed the dance in a slightly different way? Would it be the same dance?
- What is happening when you want to perform the same dance move several times?
- What term is used to create a set of instructions?
- What term is used to make decisions?

Extending this activity – where next?
Try using one of the online programming environments below to see if you can create a digital animation of the dance routine you've designed above. Games like Just Dance are great at demonstrating algorithms within the dance. Can you create your own version?

Useful related online resources
- Digital Schoolhouse – Just Dance with the Algorithm: https://www.digitalschoolhouse.org.uk/workshop/just-dance-algorithm
- Scratch, a free block-based programming environment: https://scratch.mit.edu/

- ◆ Python, a free text-based programming environment: https://www.python.org/
- ◆ Tynker, a learning programming for kids: https://www.tynker.com/

Worksheets

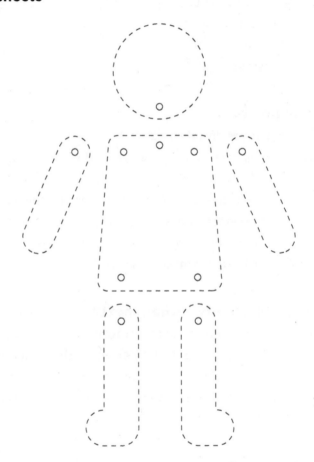

Task 1:

Choose a song and create a very simple algorithm using a flowchart or list of instructions. Remember to use **sequence, selection, iteration** and a **procedure.**

Task 2:

Move your character to the algorithm that you have created and test (debug) the routine. Why not film a video of your dance? You could share it on social media and tag @digschoolhouse on Twitter or @ DigiSchoolHouse Facebook.

Solutions

Further discussion points

1. Can dancing really be a program?
    - Yes, it is an algorithm which normally contains:
        i. **Sequence:** a set of instructions to follow in order to create the dance move correctly
        ii. **Iteration:** to loop or repeat a dance move more than once
        iii. **Procedures:** a sequence of dance moves that need to be followed
        iv. **Selection:** used to determine when the dance should start based on whether music is playing
2. What would happen if you performed the dance in a slightly different way? Would it be the same dance?
    - It would not be the same dance because the algorithm would not be in **sequence** therefore this would be known as a new algorithm.
3. What is happening when you want to perform the same dance move several times?
    - **Iteration or loops:** you are repeating several dance moves over again based on a count (how many times) or a conditional loop (until something else happens like the music stops). Iteration is another term for repetition.
4. What term is used to create a set of instructions?
    - **Algorithm:** this is the term used in programming when you make a set of instructions.
5. What term is used to make decisions?
    - **Selection:** this is the term used when programs need to make decisions, usually by IF/ELSE statements.

CHAPTER 8

. . . .

Systems Architecture

PIZZA-BOX COMPUTER

Learn the parts of a computer by making a cardboard model

What you need:

- ◆ Empty pizza box or cardboard boxes
- ◆ Colouring pens
- ◆ Paper
- ◆ String

Recommended age range:
Suitable for all ages

Prior knowledge/experience:
Must have seen personal computers at home or school

What to do

We've all seen computers, right? When we start to think about it, there are many types and shapes of computers. You may have seen a PC computer at home or at school. This could have a large screen, a keyboard, a mouse and a big box containing the components. Also, you might have a laptop computer or Chromebook, where the screen, keyboard and trackpad are all together in a folding case. Tablet computers are even more integrated with the touch screen on the front and all the components hidden inside.

A computer is a machine that processes data.

We are going to make a cardboard model of a computer. We could use empty cereal boxes for a PC, an empty pizza box to make a laptop or maybe smaller, thinner boxes for the tablet.

A PC will have a separate box for each part:

- ◆ **Screen:** a box should represent the screen, or monitor as it is also known.
- ◆ **Mouse:** this could be a small box on a piece of string, but many computer mice are wireless now.
- ◆ **Keyboard:** you could draw the keys using pens. How will you organise your letters, numbers and symbols? Can you copy a real keyboard?
- ◆ **Main box:** this box contains all the other components that work together to create the computer. The most important part of this is the Central Processing Unit (CPU). The CPU is the 'brain' of the computer.

Make your computer model and label all the parts.

Can you work out which parts are putting data IN to the computer and which parts are putting data OUT?

What you're learning

Making a model of your computer helps you recognise the parts. You will notice that a 'general purpose computer' can be used for many different tasks, including, for example, going on the web, creating a document or editing a photo. This computer can be a PC, laptop, tablet or phone, all of which contain different parts that let us INPUT data, enables the computer to PROCESS the data and then put out the data (OUTPUT). For example, you might input the data by typing on the keyboard to search the web for a video. The computer processes the instruction and then outputs the video on the monitor or screen.

Link back to the National Curriculum for Computing:
KS1
- ◆ Recognise common uses of information technology beyond school.

KS3
- ◆ Understand the hardware and software components that make up computer systems, and how they communicate with one another and with other systems.

Link back to computational thinking skills:
- ◆ This activity develops your ability to think in **abstractions.**

Extending this activity – where next?
If you have access to a digital device, then why not convert your physical model into a digital one? You can use any number of apps that are designed to handle graphics. One alternative is TinkerCad which is a Computer Aided Design package, or Blender, which also handles 3D models very well.

Useful related online resources
BBC Bitesize Primary – What are the main parts of a computer?
  https://www.bbc.com/bitesize/articles/z9myvcw
BBC Bitesize GCSE – Introducing Computers:
  https://www.bbc.com/bitesize/guides/z46s4wx/revision/1
TinkerCad – Computer Aided Design Software:
  https://www.tinkercad.com/
Blender – 3D Modelling software:
  https://www.blender.org/

ALL TOGETHER NOW

Working together like the parts of a computer
  What you need:
  ◆ Small cardboard boxes or cardboard
  ◆ Tape or gluestick
  ◆ Felt pens

Recommended age range:
Suitable for all ages

Prior knowledge/experience:
Your child must have completed the Pizza-box Computer activity

What to do

You have made a model of a computer in the previous 'Pizza-box Computer' activity. You included some important parts that you can see on the outside of the computer. What about the inside? Inside the main box, there are many important parts that need to work together.

Think about or look at a computer that you have used. It might have a DVD slot or a place to insert memory cards. There can be USB slots too on the front and back or a place to plug the computer into a socket.

The main part of the computer is the CPU, which acts as the computer's brain. Get some cardboard or a small box and draw a picture of a brain on it. Write the words Central Processing Unit (CPU) on it too. Place it inside your pizza-box computer.

Next find another box and write 'Power supply' on it.

A mobile computer (like a tablet or laptop) has a battery that can be charged. Add another box and write 'Battery'.

A computer needs to store instructions in its memory. Add a box for this and write 'Memory' on it.

More instructions and programs, such as web browsers, can be stored on a hard drive. Add another box for the 'Hard drive' and write this label on it.

The images on the screen are controlled by the 'Graphics Control Unit' or GPU. Let's add another box.

If you would like to add slots for USB connection, memory-card readers and DVD players, you can add more boxes or cut slots into the side of your pizza box.

When you have made all of the different parts, place them inside your pizza-box computer. Try and remember all the different parts.

Now, with a partner, hide one of the parts and see if they can remember what is missing. Take turns and see who can remember all of the parts and what they do.

What you're learning

Our computer model has many different parts. The **hardware** parts make up the body of the computer. On the outside there is the mouse, screen and keyboard. Inside the main box, there can be the CPU, hard drive, DVD drive, power supply and battery. All these parts or components need to work together for the computer to work. The **software** includes the instructions or programs that run on the **hardware**, to enable them to work together.

KS1

◆ Recognise common uses of information technology beyond school.

KS3

◆ Understand the hardware and software components that make up computer systems, and how they communicate with one another and with other systems.

Link back to computational thinking skills:

◆ This activity develops your ability to think in **abstractions**.

Extending this activity - where next?

Look at the digital model you created in the previous activity. Can you update it to add the additional components that you have covered in this task?

Useful related online resources

BBC Bitesize Primary – What are the main parts of a computer?
  https://www.bbc.com/bitesize/articles/z9myvcw
BBC Bitesize GCSE – Introducing Computers:
  https://www.bbc.com/bitesize/guides/z46s4wx/revision/1
TinkerCad – Computer Aided Design Software:
  https://www.tinkercad.com/
Blender – 3D Modelling software:
  https://www.blender.org/

WHAT'S IN YOUR BRAIN?

What makes up your brain and the computer's brain? Let's riddle this out!

What you need:
◆ Brain

Recommended age range:
Suitable for all ages

Prior knowledge/experience:
Your child should have completed the Pizza-box Computer and All Together Now activities

What to do

What does your brain contain? What makes up the parts of your brain?

We can put information into our brains, process it and then output information. For example, we could ask riddles with a partner. How does that work? Well, the first person can ask a riddle – this is the INPUT. The second person can PROCESS the information and try to work out the answer. The second person can say the answer to the riddle – the OUTPUT.

Now try solving some of these riddles:
1. What has a mouth and a fork, but cannot eat?
2. What has hands, but cannot clap?
3. What has to be broken before it can be heard?
4. A man drives up to a hotel and is instantly bankrupt?
5. I have many keys, but cannot open a door?

Answers: 1. a river 2. a clock 3. silence 4. playing Monopoly 5. a piano

Can you think of any more riddles?

What you're learning

Look at an image of a brain. It contains three main parts: the cerebrum, the cerebellum and the brain stem.

Parts of the brain

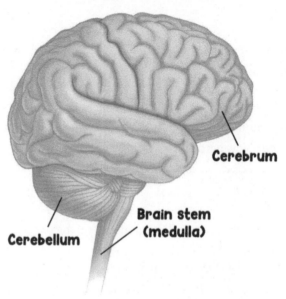

A computer's brain is the Central Processing Unit (CPU). This is made up of three parts too. The CPU contains the Control Unit (CU), Arithmetic Logic Unit (ALU) and the Memory (Registers).

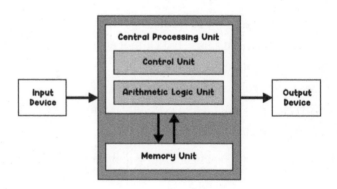

We can input information into our brains, process it and then output information. This is similar to the CPU. There is an INPUT—> PROCESS —> OUTPUT.

The PROCESS part is not simple; there is a lot going on in your brain! The same is true for the CPU. Inside the processor, the instructions are being processed by the Control Unit, Arithmetic Logic Unit and being stored and collected from the Memory Unit.

Link back to the National Curriculum for Computing:
KS1
- Recognise common uses of information technology beyond school.

KS3
- Understand the hardware and software components that make up computer systems, and how they communicate with one another and with other systems.
- Understand how instructions are stored and executed within a computer system.

Link back to computational thinking skills:
- This activity develops your ability to think in **abstractions**.

Extending this activity – where next?
Let's apply what you've learned to some of your everyday and computer-based tasks. Think about the different elements of each task. Can you break it down into its appropriate Input-Process-Output elements?

Useful related online resources
Brain diagram:
https://www.flickr.com/photos/zillafag/3284353334

Fetch! Decode! Execute! Follow the instructions in this balloon-popping game.

What you need:
- Balloons
- Paper
- Scissors
- Pens

Recommended age range:
Suitable for all ages

Prior knowledge/experience:
Your child must understand that the brain of a computer is called the processor

What to do

Do you like popping balloons? We are going to pop a lot of them now!

Think of different animals, famous people or funny sounds.

1. On a sheet of paper write a numbered list of ten animals. For example:

1. Lion
2. Horse
3. Sheep
4. Cow
5. Dog
6. Cat
7.

2. Cut a separate blank piece of paper into ten strips
3. Write the numbers one to ten on the strips, so that each strip has a different number.
4. Roll each strip of paper and place it inside a (not yet inflated) balloon.
5. Carefully, blow up each balloon and tie a knot, so that the paper is still inside.
6. Place the balloons at one end of the room.
7. Take it in turns with your child or children to run to the other end of the room, to collect a balloon (**fetch**).
8. Carefully, pop the balloon and retrieve the paper.
9. Read the number. Match the number to the animal on the list (**decode**).
10. Now, return to the start, making the sound and moving like that animal (**execute**).
11. The next person runs to collect a balloon.

Now try mixing up the game

You could vary the speed of the game by introducing a new rule. For example, if you find an odd number, then the player has to take slow, little steps. If it is an even number, then they can take quick, large steps.

Also, you could make the decoding more difficult by using foreign-language words for the numbers or even writing the list in a foreign language, so it has to be decoded (or translated) before it can be understood.

What you're learning

The Central Processing Unit (CPU) carries out instructions. To do this, it must first fetch an instruction. Secondly, it needs to decode the instruction. Then thirdly, it must carry out or execute the instruction. The catchy name for this is the fetch-execute cycle. It is called a cycle, because when it has completed the instruction, it starts again fetching a new instruction.

The reason to introduce slow, little steps or quick, large steps is to represent the 'clock speed' of a processor. A clock may make a tick-tock sound or you can see the seconds changing with a seconds hand. The clock speed is how fast the processor can work. So, a fast clock speed means it can carry out the instructions faster than one with a slower clock speed.

Link back to the National Curriculum for Computing:
KS1

◆ Recognise common uses of information technology beyond school.

KS3

◆ Understand the hardware and software components that make up computer systems, and how they communicate with one another and with other systems.
◆ Understand how instructions are stored and executed within a computer system.

Link back to computational thinking skills:
◆ This activity develops your ability to think in **abstractions**.

Extending this activity – where next?

Can you represent what you've learned in this activity as a diagram?

In reality the fetch-execute cycle is more complex than what is described here as it uses many different types of computer memory to carry out the operations that it does. Do some online research using the link below to see if you can find out more about how this works.

Useful related online resources

BBC Bitesize GCSE – the Fetch-Execute Cycle:
https://www.bbc.com/bitesize/guides/z2342hv/revision/5

It's time to get into the kitchen and get multi-tasking. This activity requires you to carry out more than one instruction at a time

What you need:

- ◆ Pens
- ◆ Paper
- ◆ Cookbook containing recipes

Recommended age range:
Suitable for all ages

Prior knowledge/experience:
Exploding Decoding activity

What to do

Have you watched a cooking programme on the TV? For example, 'The Great British Bake Off', where contestants have a cooking challenge to complete in a set time. The recipe they follow has many instructions. If they had to complete each one before going to the next, they would not finish in time. So they have to follow some of the instructions at the same time.

Think about making a cake. The oven needs to be switched on and set to a high temperature. Imagine the contestants watching the oven and waiting until it reached the correct temperature, before beginning to collect the ingredients and start making the cake mixture. This would take a long time and put them at a disadvantage in the competition. Doing more than one part at the same time can be called 'doing things in parallel'.

Another example is when you are making toast. You can put more than one slice of bread into a toaster. You don't wait for one slice to toast before taking it out and putting in the next one. You can put two pieces of bread into a toaster at the same time.

Think of your favourite item of food that you would like to cook, then look it up online or in a cookbook. You could try the Family and Kids section of the BBC Good Food website: https://www.bbcgoodfood.com/feature/family-and-kids

Look at the list of ingredients and then the cooking instructions. Can you see where more than one part or task is happening while you are doing another? Which parts of a recipe can you do in parallel?

Now you are going to plan a whole meal. Think about the different parts and put together a list of instructions to prepare the meal. For example, cooking sausages in a pan and heating up baked beans in a microwave. Which parts can you do in parallel?

What you're learning

We want to solve problems quickly. A computer has many instructions to follow and they are carried out in the processor. If a computer has two processors, then a big problem can be broken down into smaller parts and then those smaller parts can be solved at the same time, using each processor. We call this 'parallel processing'. These smaller parts are often similar and can be solved independently. Their results are then combined.

Parallel processing can also take place over a network. A very large problem can be distributed to many processors, in different computers. The sub-problems are solved and returned to the main computer program. The 'Folding@home' project is a distributed computing project for disease research. It involved modelling complex chemicals using the idle resources of computers owned by volunteers across the world. The Sony Playstation 3 was a powerful computer and games console. Parts of the medical research program were sent out to the PS3s, to solve the problems, while the games consoles were not being used. This meant the problems were being processed in parallel on many computers.

Link back to the National Curriculum for Computing:
KS1

◆ Recognise common uses of information technology beyond school.

KS3

◆ Understand the hardware and software components that make up computer systems, and how they communicate with one another and with other systems.
◆ Understand how instructions are stored and executed within a computer system.

Link back to computational thinking skills:
◆ This activity develops your ability to think in **abstractions.**

Extending this – where next?

Folding@home – Find out more about this distributed computing project and how it used PS3s for scientific research:

https://foldingathome.org/faqs/high-performance/folding-sony-playstation-3-ps3/

Useful related online resources

Kiddle Encyclopedia – Distributed Computing for Kids:
https://kids.kiddle.co/Distributed_computing
Digital Schoolhouse – Nifty Networks:
https://www.digitalschoolhouse.org.uk/documents/nifty-networks

Learn about storing instructions in the cache, in the computer's CPU

What you need:
- A4 picture of a celebrity
- Pencil
- Ruler
- Scissors
- Stopwatch
- Tray

Recommended age range:
Suitable for KS2, KS3 and KS4

Prior knowledge/experience:
Must know that the computer's brain is the CPU and that instructions are followed in the CPU

What to do

Find a large picture of a celebrity. You could print it or look in a magazine or newspaper. Can you find your favourite? You might find that using the front page of a magazine or printing your image onto card makes solving the puzzle a little easier.

You will be dividing the picture into thirty-two pieces (eight horizontally and four vertically). Use a pencil and ruler to draw horizontal lines across the picture. Can you space them equally? Now do the same with vertical lines. Have you got thirty-two pieces? Now cut them out. Take the first two rows of pieces of your image (eight pieces) and put them to one side. Mix up the rest of the pieces.

Place a tray on a table or on the floor at one end of your room. Place the eight pieces you set aside close to the tray and put the other twenty-four pieces at the other end of the room.

How quickly can you solve your jigsaw puzzle and put the picture back together again? Start the stopwatch and make your picture. You could work with another person to create a competition to see who can solve it fastest!

What you're learning

The computer's brain is the CPU. It contains registers and caches to store instructions. In our activity, the register held the first eight pieces close to the tray. Your most commonly used instructions get stored here for easy access. To illustrate this we put the first eight pieces of the picture aside to make solving the puzzle quicker. The cache is another place to store instructions. The cache can contain more instructions, but it takes longer to fetch them. That is why you needed to run to the other end of the room to collect the pieces of the picture.

INPUT –> PROCESS –> OUTPUT

You **input** the data (the pieces of jigsaw), **process** the data (decide where to put the piece to make the picture) and the **output** is the final jigsaw picture.

Link back to the National Curriculum for Computing:
KS1

◆ Recognise common uses of information technology beyond school.

KS2

◆ Solve problems by decomposing them into smaller parts.

KS3

- Understand the hardware and software components that make up computer systems, and how they communicate with one another and with other systems.
- Understand how instructions are stored and executed within a computer system.

Link back to computational thinking skills:

- This activity develops your ability to think in **abstractions**.

Extending this – where next?

Use the BBC Bitesize resource listed below to find out more about how the different types of memory work inside the CPU.

Useful related online resources

BBC Bitesize GCSE:

https://www.bbc.com/bitesize/guides/zmb9mp3/revision/1

WHAT CHORES?

Which jobs will you have to do around your home or will you escape?

What you need:

- Pens
- Paper
- Dice

Recommended age range:
Suitable for all ages

Prior knowledge/experience:
Must know that RAM stores instructions

What to do

Do you like helping around the house? Maybe you are given jobs to do, such as tidying your room, cleaning your pet's cage or helping to put the washing away. These jobs can be called 'chores'. The word 'chore' means a routine job that needs to be done (and they are not always exciting!). In the film *Mary Poppins*, the main character of the same name tried to make chores more enjoyable with the song 'A spoonful of sugar'.

Think about jobs that need doing at home and make a list. Ask a parent or adult to see if they can add to the list.

Look at your list and choose five chores. Arrange them from 1 to 5, where 1 is the easiest and 5 is the hardest. For example, 1 could be tidying up everyone's shoes and 5 could be cleaning the bathroom.

Roll a dice and see which number you get. If you roll a number 1, 2, 3, 4 or 5, then you must do that chore. However, if you roll a lucky number 6, then NO CHORES TODAY!

What you're learning

The chores or list of instructions are held in the temporary RAM memory in the computer. The dice represents the way a numbered instruction can be called up by the processor, to be executed.

Link back to the National Curriculum for Computing:
KS1

◆ Recognise common uses of information technology beyond school.

KS3

◆ Understand the hardware and software components that make up computer systems, and how they communicate with one another and with other systems.

- Understand how instructions are stored and executed within a computer system.

Link back to computational thinking skills:
- This activity develops your ability to think in **abstractions**.

Extending this activity- where next?
The next activity in the book, 'Sock It to Me!', focuses on RAM and instructions.

Useful related online resources
BBC Bitesize Revision:

　　https://www.bbc.com/bitesize/guides/zmb9mp3/revision/7

SOCK IT TO ME!

Follow the instructions to sort those socks
　　What you need:
- Socks – at least ten pairs (preferably clean)
- Pens
- Paper
- Stopwatch or timer

Recommended age range:
Suitable for all ages

Prior knowledge/experience:
Your child should have completed the What Chores activity and understand that RAM stores instructions

What to do

After the last activity, you may have thought you had finished your chores. However, we still need to sort out the washing! Albert Einstein used to have many suits, all of them the same, so he did not have to use his brain power to decide what to wear each morning. More recently, Steve Jobs, the co-founder of Apple, used to wear a dark shirt or polo-neck jumper with jeans. All these items of clothing were the same colour and style, making it easier to sort out.

How many pairs of socks do you have? Are the pairs the same or all different patterns?

Socks get mixed up in the washing and then have to be put back into pairs.

Collect ten pairs of socks and separate them, so you have twenty separate socks. Mix them up and lay them out on the floor. You can work with a partner or by yourself, using a stopwatch.

Write three lists of instructions to sort out the socks.

For example:
1. Pick a sock.
2. Look at all the other socks until you find the matching pair.
3. Place the pair together.
4. Choose another sock.

Another list of instructions could be:
1. Collect all the white socks.
2. Place the white socks in a pile.
3. Collect all the black socks.
4. Place the black socks in a pile.

5. Collect all the other coloured socks.
6. Place them in a pile.
7. Sort out each pile, so each sock finds a pair.

Maybe the instructions could be:
1. Pick two socks.
2. Start looking through all the other socks until you find the two matching pairs.
3. Pick two new socks and start matching them.

You now have three sets of instructions. With your partner or by yourself, start the stopwatch and choose a set of instructions to follow. Record the time. Keep checking that the instructions are being followed precisely.

Now try a different set of instructions and record the time. Is one method faster than the other methods?

What you're learning

Lists of instructions are held in the RAM memory in the computer. The RAM is temporary memory, so in our example you choose a set of instructions and follow them, then you forget the list and start with a new set of instructions.

Link back to the National Curriculum for Computing:
KS1

♦ Recognise common uses of information technology beyond school.

KS3

♦ Understand the hardware and software components that make up computer systems, and how they communicate with one another and with other systems.

- Understand how instructions are stored and executed within a computer system.

Link back to computational thinking skills:
- This activity develops your ability to think in **abstractions**.

Extending this activity – where next?

See if you can find out more about sort-and-search algorithms, and how they can truly make a difference. CS4FN has published a booklet that shows computational thinking in action embedded in a story about helping people with disability, even without using technology. It shows how the separate elements of computational thinking combine in interdisciplinary problem solving. Along the way it teaches some core search algorithms. It is written by Paul Curzon of Queen Mary University of London and is based on the CS4FN approach.

Can you think of any other examples of sort-and-search algorithms in play? How many can you come up with?

Useful related online resources

CS4FN – Ergo's Adventures in Thinking:
   https://teachinglondoncomputing.org/ergo/
CS4FN – 'Computational Thinking: Searching to Speak':
   https://teachinglondoncomputing.org/resources/inspiring-computing
   -stories/computational-thinking-searching-to-speak/

HOT OR COLD?

Can you find all the hidden computers?

What you need:
◆ Pens
◆ Paper

Recommended age range:
Suitable for all ages

Prior knowledge/experience:
None

What to do

Computers are hidden in objects all around our homes. For example, a television contains computers to find the programmes and display them on the screen.

Where else do you think there are hidden computers? Look around your home. There are computers in smoke alarms, microwave ovens, calculators.

Make a list of ten hidden computers you can find. Now work with a partner to help them find these computers.

Tell your partner to start moving around the room. When they get nearer a hidden computer, say 'warmer'. If they move away, say 'colder'. If they get really close, then say 'hot'. Can you help them find all ten hidden computers on your list?

What you're learning

We call these hidden computers 'embedded systems'. They are usually small computers that do a particular job. A tablet computer or desktop

PC does many jobs, such as writing letters, playing games or shopping online. The embedded system does fewer different jobs and concentrates on its particular purpose. For example, a washing machine needs to open a valve to let water into the machine. It needs to check the water is at the correct temperature, based on the programme setting. The embedded system controls the machine, doing very specific jobs.

Link back to the National Curriculum for Computing:
KS1

◆ Recognise common uses of information technology beyond school.

KS3

◆ Understand the hardware and software components that make up computer systems, and how they communicate with one another and with other systems.
◆ Understand how instructions are stored and executed within a computer system.

Link back to computational thinking skills:
◆ This activity develops your ability to think in **abstractions**.

Extending this – where next?
Think about wearable technology and Artificial Intelligence devices in the home.

Useful related online resources
Cs4FN – Artificial Intelligence . . . but where's the intelligence?:
   http://www.cs4fn.org/ai/whereistheintelligence.php
BBC Bitesize – Understanding what's inside the CPU:
   https://www.bbc.com/bitesize/guides/z46s4wx/revision/3

Spot the hidden computers around the neighbourhood, with this familiar game

What you need:

◆ Eyes

Recommended age range:
Suitable for all ages

Prior knowledge/experience:
Must have completed the Hot or Cold activity

What to do

In 'Hot or Cold' we learned about hidden computers or embedded systems around the home. There are many outside the home too. If you go to the supermarket, you will see checkouts – either with people working on them or self-scanning checkouts, where customers scan their own items. These checkouts contain embedded systems.

Do you know the game of 'I Spy'? You begin with the rhyme 'I spy with my little eye, something beginning with . . .', and then say the first letter of the object's name. We are going to do this with embedded systems. On an outdoor walk, in a supermarket, a shopping centre or cinema, play 'I Spy' with a friend. Can you see embedded systems and can your friend guess what they are?

Choose one of the objects you see and think about why it would only have a computer that does a particular job, when you could put a powerful computer in that could do many jobs?

What you're learning

Embedded systems can be found all around us. Most electrical items will contain an embedded system, a dedicated computer for specific jobs. You could put a more powerful computer into a checkout till. This would mean it could do more varied tasks than a normal checkout. For example, it could run a large spreadsheet to calculate the predicted sales that day. However, the checkout is its main purpose and it may not need to do other jobs. A more powerful computer would cost more money too.

Link back to the National Curriculum for Computing:
KS1

◆ Recognise common uses of information technology beyond school.

KS3

◆ Understand the hardware and software components that make up computer systems, and how they communicate with one another and with other systems.
◆ Understand how instructions are stored and executed within a computer system.

Link back to computational thinking skills:

◆ This activity develops your ability to think in **abstractions**.

Useful related online resources

CS4FN – Microwave Racing Activity:
   https://teachinglondoncomputing.org/resources/inspiring-unplugged
   -classroom-activities/microwave-racing-video/
Kiddle Encylopedia – Embedded Systems:
   https://kids.kiddle.co/Embedded_system

LET'S GET SMART

Predicting the future, understanding the role of smart devices around us today and the role they will continue to play in the near future

What you need:
- ◆ Eyes
- ◆ Ears

Recommended age range:
Suitable for all ages

Prior knowledge/experience:
Your child should understand what embedded systems are and what they do, and have completed the Hot or Cold and iSpy activities

What to do

We have new helpers on our phones that can talk to us. On an iPhone, you can say 'Hey, Siri'. With Google Assistant, you can say 'Hey, Google', or it can look at your diary and predict when you need to leave the house for an appointment. These can be called 'smart devices', because they appear intelligent.

In your home you may own smart devices, such as Google Home or Alexa. These devices can listen to your questions and go and find answers. They contain embedded systems to use a microphone to listen to key phrases. They are connected to the internet and take the sound of our voices and send it to large, powerful computers, where the information is processed. They can be used to control our lights, heating and electrical devices.

Imagine the future. Will these smart devices be embedded in every object of your home?

Design a comic of the future on a sheet of paper. What will the future look like? What will the smart devices in the objects do? For example, would a washing machine be voice-activated?

Could there be a problem with smart devices? What could go wrong? Or will they make everyone's lives easier?

What you're learning

Smart devices contain embedded systems. They connect to powerful computers, via the internet. They can appear intelligent because they respond in a human manner. Alan Turing was a computer scientist in the 1950s. He developed a test to see if a machine could 'think'. In the test a machine or computer is asked questions and a human has to decide whether they are talking to another human or a machine.

Activity

What do you think about Siri, Alexa, Cortana or Google? Do they seem human to you? If you have access to one of these smart devices, then try having a conversation with them the way you would with your friend. At what point in the conversation can you tell that you're talking to a device rather than another human being? What were you talking about? Can you find the best way to test this out on a device that you have access to?

Link back to the National Curriculum for Computing:
KS1

- ◆ Recognise common uses of information technology beyond school.

KS3

- Understand the hardware and software components that make up computer systems, and how they communicate with one another and with other systems.
- Understand how instructions are stored and executed within a computer system.

Link back to computational thinking skills:

- This activity develops your ability to think in **abstractions**.

Extending this – where next?

Think about wearable technology and the development of Artificial Intelligence devices.

Useful related online resources

Wikipedia – Find out more about the Turing Test:
https://en.wikipedia.org/wiki/Turing_test
BBC News – Can machines think:
https://www.bbc.co.uk/news/technology-18475646

CHAPTER 9

Safety and Security

TWENTY-ONE QUESTIONS

Learn about security through a game of Twenty-One Questions

What you need:

- ◆ Pen
- ◆ Paper

Recommended age range:
Suitable for all ages

Prior knowledge/experience:
None required

What to do

The purpose of this activity is to teach the child that they need to be careful about what answers they give to questions. Sometimes people may ask seemingly innocent questions, but the answer could give away personal information, or the questioner could slip in probing or personal questions and catch you off guard. This could be applied to any situation, but the main focus is on when children have contact with people online. This may be on social media, but could also be in chat rooms, forums, etc.

The game is simple. You ask your child twenty-one questions. They can decide not to answer, or pass, on two of them, but need to answer the other questions. If they don't think they should answer the question but haven't got any passes left, they must either ask to come back to the question later or make something up (this could be a difficult moment as we all teach our children not to lie, but sometimes if it is to protect ourselves, a little white lie is better than giving all our personal details away).

Try to get your child to write the answers down as you ask them as well as answering them verbally, but if this will take too long just get them to answer verbally.

Here are the questions. You can obviously change some of them to other questions if you wish:

- What is your favourite song at the moment?

- Do you think the convenience of technology is worth the loss of privacy that comes with it?

- Is it okay to sacrifice one life to save ten? If you said yes, would you change your answer if the one life was a friend's life and the ten were strangers? If no, why not?

- What do most people think about you that is absolutely not true?

- What are the consequences of everyone having instant distraction at their fingertips?

- What should they teach you in school but don't?

- What is your favourite film or book?

- Who would you most like to sit next to on a ten-hour flight and why?

- What are two things you think you should know how to do but don't?

- Tell me about your favourite pet?

- You have £100 to spend, all your friends are busy and you have the whole day to yourself, what do you do?

- What is the most memorable thing that has happened to you in your life so far?

- How much do you change when you know no one is around?

- How much do you know about the world outside your country?

- What is your favourite hobby?

- If you see a homeless person asking for money, should you give them any?

- How adventurous are you? Give some examples.

- Who do you want to be more like?

- Do you think any part of your personality needs to be improved? If so, which part and why?

- What is the strangest habit you have?

The answers to all the questions tell you something about the person. What question would you ask? Add the twenty-first question to this list.

After you have asked all the questions and they have been answered, get your child to think about some of their answers.

Were there any questions that directly asked for personal details? Where there any that didn't directly ask for personal details, but they did give out personal information in their answers?

Were there any answers that people could use, for example to try your favourite song or pet's name as a password?

Which questions did they decide to pass on and why? Did these questions make them feel uncomfortable or did they not want to give out an answer or did they just not know what to say or know what the question was asking?

Point out to them that they do need to think about any answers they give out to people online or offline and think about what they are being asked and why.

What you're learning

This activity helps you to learn how seemingly 'harmless' or generic questions can give out a fair amount of personal details. If this information was being given out online then it could be used by someone to carry out identity fraud. They could use the information to try and guess your password or answers to your key security questions. It is always important to be mindful of the information that we are sharing in an online environment as well as being very careful about what passwords we choose and what we set our security questions to be.

Link back to the National Curriculum for Computing: KS2

♦ Understand a range of ways to use technology safely, respectfully, responsibly and securely, including protecting their online identity and privacy.

Useful online resources

Digital Schoolhouse – Guess Who (online safety):
https://www.digitalschoolhouse.org.uk/documents/guess-who

HOME SECURITY CHECK

Learning about the need for security when using digital devices by doing a security exercise in the home

What you need:
- ◆ Your home
- ◆ Pen and paper

Recommended age range:
Suitable for all ages

Prior Knowledge/Experience:
None required

What to do

The adult must go around the home beforehand and make sure there are some security breaches. These should include an external door that isn't locked; a window that is left open; leaving a digital device on, facing out of a window where it can be seen (if this is possible) with the internet enabled and displayed on the screen.

Once it is set up the adult should tell the child that they need to go around the house and look for things that need checking to make sure they are locked and/or shut as if everyone in the home was going out.

The child must try to find the security breaches and write them down on a sheet of paper. The adult can accompany them and help if necessary (you could use the 'hot or cold' approach here).

Once all the breaches have been found, discuss why security is important. Then link this with digital devices: why do we need to have things such as security pins to lock devices and passwords to log into devices and different accounts? Also discuss visible security such as keeping screens away from windows or covering screens up in public places. You could introduce the example of hiding your PIN numbers at cashpoints and at tills in shops.

Discuss WiFi and the importance of password-protected access so that other people can't access their WiFi and access their devices. Discuss the importance of keeping physical keys safe and knowing how many there are and where they are.

What you're learning

This simple activity helps to highlight the importance of security for children. Understanding physical security needs such as ensuring doors and windows are locked before leaving the house is easier for children to be able to understand. The activity brings this to the forefront of their minds. The follow-on discussion then helps translate the importance of security to our digital lives. Passwords and passcodes are not that dissimilar to locks on our doors and windows. Depending on the age of the children and their access to digital devices it would be useful to sit down with them and discuss what possible security measures could be applied and where.

Link back to the National Curriculum for Computing: KS1

- ◆ Use technology safely and respectfully, keeping personal information private; identify where to go for help and support when they have concerns about content or contact on the internet or other online technologies.

KS2

♦ Use technology safely, respectfully and responsibly; recognise acceptable/unacceptable behaviour; identify a range of ways to report concerns about content and contact.

KS3

♦ Understand a range of ways to use technology safely, respectfully, responsibly and securely, including protecting their online identity and privacy; recognise inappropriate content, contact and conduct, and know how to report concerns.

Extending this – where next?

Setting up passwords. What types of digital accounts might the child need a password for? What does a good password look like? Can they come up with a secure password? There are a common set of recommendations for coming up with strong passwords – can they find out what they are?

It would be a good idea to discuss fire security with the child as an extension. Start by looking for fire hazards and thinking what we might have in the home or could buy to help with fire safety – smoke alarms, CO_2 alarms, fire blankets and so on. Then work out fire escape routes from each room in the house, especially the child's bedroom, and what the child should do if ever there was a fire in the home.

Useful related online resources

Think You Know – Online Safety resources divided into age-suitable categories for your child and for you:
    https://www.thinkuknow.co.uk/
NSPCC – Keeping children safe online:
    https://www.nspcc.org.uk/preventing-abuse/keeping-children-safe
    /online-safety/

Police – Preventing burglary:

https://www.police.uk/crime-prevention-advice/burglary/

Fire Service – Fire safety advice:

https://www.fireservice.co.uk/safety/

YOU CAN'T DO THAT

Develop understanding of different access levels and why they are needed

What you need:

- Pens
- Paper

Recommended age range:
Suitable for all ages

Prior knowledge/experience:
Your child should have completed the Home Security Check activity

---

What to do

Ask your child to think of things that they *can't* do at home that you *can* do. You might want to give them a couple of examples to help them get started. These may include opening a medicine cupboard (if it is up high or locked), answering the front door, using the kettle, etc. Once they have the idea get them to write down as many examples as they can think of. You should be able to link some of it back to the Home Security Check.

Go through their list and discuss why they may not be able to do it, but you can. For example:

- Medicine cupboard: you know what the medicines are for and what dosage is needed and by whom, but they don't and so could end up seriously ill if they took the wrong medicine (or too much).
- Boiling the kettle: they may not be old enough to handle vessels full of boiling water safely.

Hopefully they will have covered things such as downloading apps on a phone, filtered content on the internet, filtered TV services, different users on a device.

Discuss these last points even if they haven't thought of them.

Start simple: why have different users on devices? Sometimes it's about keeping information separate (for example, you might not allow anyone to use your work laptop). Or it may be so that different users can find personalised content that interests them and also to restrict access to certain unsuitable things. If you use Netflix, discuss the advantages of having different users. Discuss how this allows Netflix to customise programmes to certain tastes and genres, for example children's films; show the user what they were last watching; allow them to choose favourites, and so on.

Discuss apps. Some aren't suitable for their age group as the content may contain offensive material. As parents you might want to check them out first. The conversation can follow on from here to broader internet content, TV filtering, etc.

This is a good point to begin a discussion around suitable and unsuitable content. Perhaps you could establish some family rules if you haven't done so already, or if you have then revisit why they are important.

What you're learning

This activity builds upon children's existing understanding of why they are not allowed to do certain things. They know that adults have access to everything, and as children their own is limited. If they have older siblings they may also appreciate that their 'access levels' will increase according to age. It is then a simple step to translate this into the digital world and understand the importance of setting access rights on various devices. You may for example, as a parent, use this as an opportunity to begin to discuss the parental controls available on devices and games consoles. Why are these important? You may choose to look at the options and set them together.

Link back to the National Curriculum for Computing:
KS1

 ◆ Use technology safely and respectfully, keeping personal information private; identify where to go for help and support when they have concerns about content or contact on the internet or other online technologies.

KS2

 ◆ Use technology safely, respectfully and responsibly; recognise acceptable/unacceptable behaviour; identify a range of ways to report concerns about content and contact.

KS3

 ◆ understand a range of ways to use technology safely, respectfully, responsibly and securely, including protecting their online identity and privacy; recognise inappropriate content, contact and conduct, and know how to report concerns.

Useful related online resources

Childnet – Broad advice about safe use of technology:
https://www.childnet.com/parents-and-carers
Ask About Games – Advice for parents on family gaming and staying safe online:
https://www.askaboutgames.com/

CAESAR CIPHER

Sending messages secretly using the Caesar cipher
What you need:
◆ Pen
◆ Paper

Recommended age range:
Suitable for all ages, but works best with children who have at least basic literacy skills

Prior knowledge/experience:
No prior knowledge required

What to do

The Caesar cipher, named after Roman Emperor Julius Caesar, is one of the earliest and most widely known ciphers. It is a simple form of a 'substitution cipher', where you replace each letter of the alphabet with another letter by shifting the whole alphabet a certain number of letters. For example, this would be your key and code if you shift each letter by five spaces:

Plain	A	B	C	D	E	F	G	H	I	J	K	L	M	N	O	P	Q	R	S	T	U	V	W	X	Y	Z
Cipher	V	W	X	Y	Z	A	B	C	D	E	F	G	H	I	J	K	L	M	N	O	P	Q	R	S	T	U

So, when you write your message, the letter A gets replaced with V, B gets replaced with W and so on. For example, the word HELLO reads:

Plain: HELLO
Cipher: CZGGJ

In order to decode your message, you need to share the 'key' – the number five – with the person who needs to decode the message.

Method

- Explain the concept of a Caesar cipher to the child
- Write down the alphabet from A to Z.
- Pick a number from one to twenty-five. (If you use twenty-six, you will just wind up with the original alphabet.) This number is your key.
- Shift the entire alphabet by the number you picked and write it down below your original alphabet (as shown previously).
- Pick a message to write to your child. It might be easiest to start out with a simple message (such as a single word or phrase) before you try longer sentences or paragraphs.
- Write down your encoded message using your shifted alphabet. If it helps, write down your plain text message first then encode it one letter at a time (such as the 'HELLO' example above). Just make sure the piece of paper you give your child only has the encoded message!
- Give your child the encoded message and give them the key. Discuss why you wouldn't want to write down the key.
- See if your child can decrypt your message. If it helps for the first try, let them work backwards using the original and

shifted alphabets you wrote down. Using the example from the background, the letter V becomes A, X becomes B, and so on.

- ◆ Try switching and using a different key for the same messages. Do either look easier to crack?

What you're learning

Cryptography and encryption have long since been a method by which we have kept messages secure during transit and away from prying eyes. What topic is your child studying in school? Is their latest topic the Romans or the Tudors? If so, then this can tie in very nicely with what they are learning in history at school.

Modern encryption is fundamentally based upon complex mathematical algorithms and has widespread use. From personal email accounts to government communications, a lot of digital tools now have encryption built into them. When covering this activity, this is a good opportunity to begin talking about data privacy and its importance in our lives.

Link back to the National Curriculum for Computing:
KS1

- ◆ Use technology safely and respectfully, keeping personal information private; identify where to go for help and support when they have concerns about content or contact on the internet or other online technologies.

KS2

- ◆ Use technology safely, respectfully and responsibly; recognise acceptable/unacceptable behaviour; identify a range of ways to report concerns about content and contact.

- Understand a range of ways to use technology safely, respectfully, responsibly and securely, including protecting their online identity and privacy; recognise inappropriate content, contact and conduct, and know how to report concerns.

Extending this – where next?

- Ask another person, who does not know what a Caesar cipher is, to 'intercept' your message and try to crack your code. Can they do it?
- Discuss whether or not you think the Caesar cipher is sophisticated enough to use any more? Caesar ciphers are very vulnerable when the decoder simply tries each possible combination of letters. This might take a while for humans, but modern computers would crack the code in milliseconds.
- Could you teach your child to crack the Caesar cipher using frequency analysis, which is based on the fact that in natural English speech and writing certain letters appear much more frequently than others. For example, the letter E appears more often than any other one, whereas Z appears the least often. Imagine you read an entire paragraph and notice that the letter C appears more often than any other, odds are that it used a Caesar cipher with a shift of two (making the letter E a C in the code). This technique will be more accurate for longer blocks of text and very inaccurate for short words or phrases because there are plenty of words that do not contain an E at all. Can you give your child an entire paragraph with a Caesar cipher and then ask them to crack it using frequency analysis?

- In order to prevent someone cracking the code you could regularly change the key, for example using a new one every week. This is a similar concept to periodically changing your computer passwords.

Useful related online resources

CS4FN – Cyber security in the movies:
  http://www.cs4fn.org/security/movies/

Imperial War Museum – Secret activities to do at home:
  https://www.iwm.org.uk/sites/default/files/public-document/Secret%20Activities.pdf

Digital Schoolhouse – Cryptography: Secrets, Secrets, Secrets (aimed at teachers in schools but can be adapted for home):
  https://www.digitalschoolhouse.org.uk/workshops/cryptography-secrets-secrets-secrets-everyone-has-them

---

MASTERMIND

Try to crack the number code using the classic Mastermind game

What you need:
- Pen
- Paper
- Mastermind board, provided on the last page of this section

Recommended age range:
Suitable for all ages

Prior knowledge/experience:
Must know what a Caesar cipher is

What to do

Let's learn about code breaking by having a game of Mastermind.

What is Mastermind?

Mastermind is a code-breaking game for two players.

1. One person selects four numbers between one and nine and writes them down at the bottom of the board, or on a separate piece of paper if that is easier. Keep the numbers a secret by hiding them from the guesser. The four numbers are called a string.
2. The other player guesses the string of four by writing four numbers in the boxes in the 'Guess 1' row.
3. In the four boxes to the right of the guess the first player then gives clues to how well the other has done. These are:
   a. A shaded square which means that letter or number is correct and in the correct place.
   b. An empty square means that the number is correct but in the incorrect place.
   c. A blank space which means that the number is not correct.
4. If the second player hasn't guessed all four correctly, they have a second guess.
5. The game then continues until the second player guesses all four numbers correctly and in the correct order, in which case they win. If they don't guess them all with twelve guesses, the first player wins.

Method

Explain the rules to your child. It may be difficult to understand so you might want to have a run-through go first until they get the idea.

Decide who is going to go first.

They then write down their four number choices in the boxes in the answer row at the bottom of the sheet.

The other player then writes down their first guess in the top row.

The second player then fills in the four small squares to let the guesser know how many they have got right and in the right place, right but in the wrong place or not right at all.

In the example below the first player would draw a shaded square because five has been guessed correctly and is in the right place and an empty square as four is a correct number, but is in the wrong place. The other two boxes are left blank as neither seven nor nine were correct numbers.

					■	□
Guess 1	5	7	4	9		
Answer	5	4	2	1		

The guesser then has a second guess and the process repeats. The skill in the game comes from using logic and some lucky guessing to pinpoint which number is correct and in the right position and then which number was right, but in the wrong position (and therefore will need moving), and which numbers are wrong and can therefore be discarded from the game.

Once the string has been guessed – or if it hasn't been correctly identified after twelve guesses – the players swap over.

To make it into a longer game agree to have a certain number of rounds. It must be an equal number so that each player guesses and sets the number the same amount of times as their opponent. The codemaker gets one point for each guess a codebreaker makes. An extra point is earned by the codemaker if the codebreaker doesn't guess the pattern exactly in the last guess. The winner is the one who has the most points after the agreed-upon number of rounds are played.

What you're learning

There are software programs that are designed to break codes. They have built-in functions where the program looks for patterns and enters different combinations at a speed much faster than humans can process. The program learns as it works through the combinations, and therefore is eventually able to crack the code. You can argue that all codes are breakable, it's just a matter of how long the computer will take to crack it. That's why it's so important to have strong passwords, and combinations with more complex patterns, because the computer is less likely to crack the code within a useful time period.

Link back to the National Curriculum for Computing:
KS1

♦ Use technology safely and respectfully, keeping personal information private; identify where to go for help and support when they have concerns about content or contact on the internet or other online technologies.

KS2

♦ Use technology safely, respectfully and responsibly; recognise acceptable/unacceptable behaviour; identify a range of ways to report concerns about content and contact.

KS3

- ◆ Understand the hardware and software components that make up computer systems, and how they communicate with one another and with other systems.
- ◆ Understand how instructions are stored and executed within a computer system; understand how data of various types (including text, sounds and pictures) can be represented and manipulated digitally, in the form of binary digits.
- ◆ Understand a range of ways to use technology safely, respectfully, responsibly and securely, including protecting their online identity and privacy; recognise inappropriate content, contact and conduct, and know how to report concerns.

Extending this activity – where next?

Why not put some of your programming skills into practice and see if you can create a digital version of this? You could use an environment such as Scratch, Python, Construct 3 or any other you find that's suitable.

Useful related online resources

Why not try a simple version using colours (as used in the original game) at https://scratch.mit.edu/projects/119226130/

Mastermind Board

Guess 1					
Guess 2					
Guess 3					
Guess 4					
Guess 5					
Guess 6					
Guess 7					
Guess 8					
Guess 9					
Guess 10					
Guess 11					
Guess 12					
Answer					

PACKET SNIFFING

Learn about packet switching by sniffing out chocolate hidden in envelopes.

What you need:

◆ Three different types of small chocolate bars
◆ Twelve envelopes, each big enough to take two pieces of chocolate

Recommended age range:
Suitable for all ages

Prior knowledge/experience:
None required

What to do

1. Let your child sniff each chocolate bar to get an idea of what they smell like. Once they have done this break the bars into pieces and share the pieces of each bar between four envelopes (do not mix the chocolate bars up, you should have four envelopes of each type of chocolate).
2. Repeat this so that you have twelve envelopes all with chocolate in them.
3. Seal the envelopes so the chocolate won't come out and can't be seen. Mix the envelopes up.
4. Let your child smell each envelope, one at a time, and sort them into three separate piles. One pile for each type of chocolate. Can they name them?
5. Once they have done this open the envelopes up. If they have managed to get four envelopes in the same pile with exactly the same chocolate in them, they get to eat the chocolate. If they have

managed more than one, they should obviously share with you! If they haven't managed to do any, then let them have another go until they get it right.

Ask them to think about furniture when it is delivered. Packages come in all sorts of different shapes and sizes. It is the same with data on computers – sometimes we get text, other times images or videos. Most are too large to send all in one packet, so we break them up into smaller packets. Imagine if we sent them over the internet with no labels to say what they are? What do you think would happen?

Now try this
- ◆ Repeat step 1 above. You may want to start again with fresh chocolate bars or put the originals – if they haven't been eaten – back in the envelopes.
- ◆ Now get some other family members involved and spread out across the room.
- ◆ Designate one family member at the other end of the room to receive the chocolate. Can they open the envelopes for only one type of chocolate? So, for example, if you had a Twix bar, Cadbury's Whole Nut and a bar of Galaxy Chocolate, can they open up only the envelopes with the Twix pieces in them?
- ◆ Mix it up:
  - ○ Family member 1 wants a Twix
  - ○ Family member 2 wants the bar of Whole Nut
  - ○ Family member 3 wants the bar of Galaxy
- ◆ How can you make sure that each family member gets only the envelopes containing the chocolate that they need? Additional information is required. But what information is this? Allow plenty of opportunity for discussion and try out as many different scenarios as you can, even if

they don't look like they'll work. Your child will learn from the trial-and-error element.

- ◆ Essentially, you'd need the following items of information written as labels on the envelopes:
  - ○ Name of chocolate
  - ○ Who the recipient is
  - ○ The packet number
  - ○ Total number of packets to expect

What you're learning

When computers send packets of information over networks (i.e. the Internet), each packet has the following information sent with it:

- ◆ Recipient address, normally an IP address (a unique identifier for an internet-enabled device)
- ◆ Title of the file
- ◆ How many packets of information make up the file
- ◆ What part of the file the packet is so it can be put back into the right order. For example it might be the eleventh packet of forty-five

It will then have the actual part of the file that is being sent. These packets make their own way through the internet to their destination and then the device at the receiving end will put the packets back together to form the whole file.

What is packet sniffing? And how is this related to security?

Packet sniffing is the act of capturing a data packet that is being sent across a computer network. It is similar to what you might see in the movies when they 'wiretap' a telephone line (network). Packet sniffing is mostly used by hackers who are illegally collecting information about the network.

Internet Service Providers (ISPs) use packet sniffing to track all your activities such as:

- ◆ Who are you sending your email to?
- ◆ What is inside the email?
- ◆ What are you downloading?
- ◆ What websites do you visit?
- ◆ What do you look for on that website?
- ◆ Did you download anything from that website?
- ◆ Do you stream video? If so, what?

Link back to the National Curriculum for Computing:
KS2

- ◆ Understand computer networks, including the internet; how they can provide multiple services, such as the World Wide Web, and the opportunities they offer for communication and collaboration.

KS3

- ◆ Understand the hardware and software components that make up computer systems, and how they communicate with one another and with other systems.
- ◆ Understand how instructions are stored and executed within a computer system; understand how data of various types (including text, sounds and pictures) can be represented and manipulated digitally, in the form of binary digits.

Useful related online resources

Watch this video:

https://www.youtube.com/watch?v=ewrBalT_eBM

WHAT CAN I FIND OUT ABOUT MUM AND DAD ONLINE?

This activity will help develop an awareness of the importance of restricting the information we give away online by thinking about what we post and locking our accounts down

What you need:
- ◆ Internet-enabled device
- ◆ Smartphone

Recommended age range:
Suitable for all ages

Prior knowledge/experience:
None

What to do

Adults may want to do this exercise for themselves first to make sure there are no unsuitable things that the child might find. If you find anything unsuitable, make sure it is removed before doing this activity with your child. Check that you have the privacy settings for your social media profiles updated and set how you want them – you may wish to set them all to private. You will also need to decide how many different websites you want to restrict it to.

The child should simply be told that they have five minutes to see what information they can find about Mum or Dad (or both) online. This should be done on an account that isn't completely locked down so that things like Facebook and other social media sites can be looked at.

The adult needs to sit with the child as they are doing this exercise so that they can discuss what they find and point them to as many different things as possible so that the child realises the breadth of where information may go.

Start with a Google search. Go through the first page of search results. If there are social media accounts, then look at these. Even if they are locked down it may be that posts from other people are shown.

Discuss what should and shouldn't be posted to social media, and remember to talk about the minimum age requirements for specific sites and apps – for example, as of February 2019 you must be thirteen years of age to have a Facebook account. Look at all the different websites that your parents are on. It may be that you narrow the search by adding the town that you live in or the company that you work for. Discuss how each entry may have come about and what could be done if we wanted to get it removed.

If other social media sites appear, go through minimum ages and different settings if applicable (and change the existing ones if need be). If social media accounts are locked, you could go to the website and search for an account that isn't private and look at it and discuss why you might want to make it private. Simply go to Instagram.com and search for a common name such as Dave – there are lots of open accounts to look at.

What you're learning

Most people nowadays have an online presence with at least one if not several social media accounts. We post aspects of our lives and daily activity and can easily forget that the data being uploaded now exists almost permanently on the internet. This activity raises that awareness amongst our children, and provides an opportunity for family discussion centred around privacy and what is or isn't acceptable to post and share online.

Link back to the National Curriculum for Computing:
KS1

 ◆ Use technology purposefully to create, organise, store, manipulate and retrieve digital content.

KS2

◆ Use search technologies effectively, appreciate how results are selected and ranked, and be discerning in evaluating digital content.

KS3

◆ Understand a range of ways to use technology safely, respectfully, responsibly and securely, including protecting their online identity and privacy.

Useful related online resources

Think U Know – How to stay safe online, with age-appropriate resources: https://www.thinkuknow.co.uk/

NSPCC – Keeping Children Safe Online: https://www.nspcc.org.uk/preventing-abuse/keeping-children-safe /online-safety/

WHAT MAKES A STRONG PASSWORD?

Develop knowledge of what makes a strong password through a keyword game

What you need:

◆ Pen

◆ Paper

Recommended age range:
Suitable for all ages

Prior knowledge/experience:
Should have completed the What Can I Find Out About Mum and Dad Online? activity

---

What to do

Ask your child to write down twenty words they associate most with you. Hopefully they will come up with your name, your date of birth, where you live, pet's name, sporting team you support, favourite TV star, favourite app, etc.

Go through the list with them. Then get them to imagine that someone can find this information about you on the internet. You could take them on to the internet to look for this information or, if you have already completed it, you may have found this information during the What Can I Find Out About Mum and Dad activity.

Ask your child to write down five possible passwords they think you might have. Did they manage to identify any of your passwords correctly? If so, you will now need to change them. Discuss how you could create a strong password, using the example of a date of birth. For example, 16/04/2005 could be 16April2005, which is stronger as it has a capital letter in it. Discuss ways of making it even stronger. Here are some examples:

6teenapr1l2005
164pril2005
16@pril2005
16#apR#2005

Discuss what makes a strong password. This should include:

- At least eight characters
- At least one capital letter
- At least one number
- At least one special character e.g. #, @, _

You could get them to think about using a sentence if it would be easier for them to remember, e.g. My3petssupport#astonvilla

What you're learning

Maintaining sensible, strong passwords and being secure about keeping them confidential is a necessary skill in today's digital world. Passwords should be robust and secure in order to try and prevent us becoming victims of crimes such as identity fraud.

Link back to the National Curriculum for Computing:

KS1

- ◆ Use technology purposefully to create, organise, store, manipulate and retrieve digital content.

KS2

- ◆ Use search technologies effectively, appreciate how results are selected and ranked, and be discerning in evaluating digital content.

KS3

- ◆ Understand a range of ways to use technology safely, respectfully, responsibly and securely, including protecting their online identity and privacy.

Extending this – where next?

Reverse the exercise: your child could write down some strong passwords of their own and see whether you can crack them.

Why not go online and try some passwords out on:
https://howsecureismypassword.net/

Useful related online resources

Think U Know – How to stay safe online, with age-appropriate resources:
https://www.thinkuknow.co.uk/
NSPCC – Keeping Children Safe Online:
https://www.nspcc.org.uk/preventing-abuse/keeping-children-safe/online-safety/

Conclusion

Can you teach the computing curriculum without using a computer at all?

Yes, and that's what we've done in this book. No doubt, to be able to develop real skill and proficiency in computer programming, graphics design, network engineering and many other jobs in computers and technology, you will absolutely need to use a machine with the right tools and resources available. However, the activities in this book introduce the key concept areas for each aspect of the computing curriculum throughout the key stages. It is only through understanding the concepts inherent within the computing discipline that we are then able to develop the practical and technical skills that we need to achieve true mastery over the subject.

Technical experts are exactly what we need in order to meet the growing demand from industry to fill job roles. As technology develops, new jobs are being created all the time. Today's students could end up being a VR worlds developer, or a VR host, or how about a machine learning engineer or a computer vision researcher. Only a few short years ago these jobs simply did not exist, and now they are among hundreds of similar roles that run the risk of remaining unfulfilled if we fail to develop our own homegrown talent.

What's stopping our children from choosing to follow a career in the tech sector as they grow older? That is a question that has been debated time and again, and there are clearly numerous factors for us to consider. However, two things are certainly clear. Firstly, children cannot aspire to careers that they don't know exist; and secondly, very few, if any, children are going to aspire to a career they see as being inaccessible or unenjoyable.

So how can we open the door to a world of opportunities? There are any number of activities for children to engage in and lots of these opportunities are open for schools at little to no cost. Take, for example, the Digital Schoolhouse annual esports tournament that uses the medium of esports as an immersive careers education tool. Students take part in a number of roles to work together to organise an esports tournament, all the while getting direct access to industry.

The key here is *fun* and removing the misconceptions that surround computing. Computing is not a dry subject that is too technical for most of us to grasp. Tackled correctly it can be engaging and accessible for all children. Hopefully, the playful approach taken in this book will have helped you to understand that for yourselves. The playful and explorative nature of activities in this book helps to develop not only a child's under-standing of computing, but also a broader set of soft skills. Creativity and problem-solving are key here, along with communication, innovative thinking, algorithmic thinking, critical and computational thinking and communication. These are all key competencies that our children will need in order to succeed in the twenty-first century.[5]

Allowing children time to focus, encouraging a play-based learning approach, breaking down learning into smaller chunks and fostering reflective reasoning and analysis are among the many strategies recommended by the World Economic Forum in their New Vision for Education report.

5 World Economic Forum; New Vision for Education (2015), https://www.weforum.org/agenda/2016/03/21st-century-skills-future-jobs-students/

If you take anything away from this book, it should be a sense of fun and exploration as a medium for learning. Through an understanding of the digital tools around us we can find ways to use them not only to get a better understanding of our world but also to help arrive at solutions to make tomorrow's world a better place to live. Often our biggest obstacle is our own fear and lack of confidence; it's important that we provide our children with the confidence; to develop the skills they are going to need for tomorrow.

Don't be afraid to design your own activities. Remember, you can teach programming concepts and games design through a simple game of snap, or you could pick up some Play-Doh and teach debugging and algorithmic thinking.

Remember, no idea is too crazy!

Useful Links and Resources

There are lots of free resources available online that you can use to support your child's education in computing. You don't have to spend a penny to participate with any of the materials listed below; the only thing you will need is access to a web browser to get you started.

Name	Description	URL
BBC Webwise	A–Z glossary of computing terms, with links to relevant resources to explain the concept.	http://www.bbc.co.uk/webwise/a-z/
A bit of cs4fn	Puzzles, magazines and activities that allow you to explore computational thinking and computer science concepts away from the computer. Suitable for primary school students, Key Stage 1 and 2.	https://abitofcs4fn.org/
BAFTA YGD	Run by BAFTA Games, this is a free-to-enter games design competition for ten to eighteen year olds.	http://ygd.bafta.org/
BBC Bitesize	Developed by the BBC, this highly regarded resource seeks to explain all aspects of the computing curriculum. Short animated videos explain key concepts nicely for all students aged five to sixteen.	https://www.bbc.co.uk/bitesize

BBC Micro:Bit	Micro:bit is a tiny affordable programmable computer. The website contains an online emulator if you don't have the device at home, allowing you to practise programming in multiple environments.	https://microbit.org/code/
Beanz: The Magazine for Kids, Code and Computer Science	Fairy tales, articles, puzzles and more to help children understand computing concepts.	https://www.kidscodecs.com/loops-a-fairy-tale/
Code Combat	CodeCombat is a game-based computer science program where students type real code and see their characters react in real time.	https://codecombat.com/
Code.org	Hours of free code activities to try. All you need is your web browser.	https://code.org/
Code Avengers	Free interactive courses and tutorials to teach programming.	https://www.codeavengers.com/
Construct 3	Something for the older children, a game develop-ment environment that allows you to program your game using block-based code or JavaScript.	https://editor.construct.net/
CS4FN	Computer Science for Fun, developed by Queen Mary, University of London, is a resource that presents tradi-tional computer science concepts in fun accessible ways. There are lots of read-ing materials and activities that can be downloaded here.	http://www.cs4fn.org/

CyberFirst	Girls competition run by the National Cyber Security Centre to inspire the next generation of young women to consider a career in cyber security.	https://www.ncsc.gov.uk/cyberfirst/overview
Game Maker	A free game development tool that allows you to make your own games without coding.	https://www.yoyogames.com/gamemaker
Internet Live Stats	Live statistics of what's happening on the internet right now.	https://www.internetlivestats.com
Khan Academy	Suitable for older children and adults, learn about computing.	https://www.khanacademy.org/computing/
Scratch	Online block-based programming environment for children. Popular in primary schools.	https://scratch.mit.edu/

Index